CRIMINAL JURISDICTION UNDER THE UNITED STATES-PHILIPPINE MILITARY BASES AGREEMENT

CRIMINAL JURISDICTION UNDER THE UNITED STATES-PHILIPPINE MILITARY BASES AGREEMENT

A STUDY IN CONJURISDICTIONAL LAW

by

JOSEPH W. DODD

Department of Political Science
The University of Tennessee

MARTINUS NIJHOFF / THE HAGUE / 1968

ISBN 978-94-015-0043-2 ISBN 978-94-015-0518-5 (eBook)
DOI 10.1007/978-94-015-0518-5

TO MY MOTHER AND FATHER

TABLE OF CONTENTS

ACKNOWLEDGMENTS

The collection of material for this study was greatly facilitated by the assistance of a number of people. I would like to thank Mr. Lewis C. Coffin, Law Librarian, Library of Congress; Mr. David M. Valderrama, Hispanic Law Division, Library of Congress; Dr. Sung Yoon Cho, Far Eastern Law Division, Library of Congress; Mr. Abdul Rony, Acting Head, South Asia Section, Orientalia Division, Library of Congress; Miss Anna Wood, Head, Government Documents Department, Howard-Tilton Library, Tulane University; Lieutenant Colonel Robert B. Ellert, Chief, Status of Forces Branch, Office of the Judge Advocate General, Department of the Army; Captain Geoffrey E. Carlisle, Director, International Law Division, Office of the Judge Advocate General, Department of the Navy; and Mr. Eugene T. Herbert, Office of the Legal Adviser, Department of State. I am also grateful to Colonel Earl A. Morgan, Chief, International Law Division, Office of the Judge Advocate General, Department of the Air Force, who made available *OCS Form 782* and *JAG Form 66.* I owe a particular debt of gratitude to the following legal officers in the field: Captain Richard J. Hackett, Director of International Law, Clark Air Base; Commander W. J. Davis, Legal Officer, Sangley Point Naval Station; and Captain Nathan Cole, Jr., Staff Legal Officer, Subic Bay Naval Base. Their prompt correspondence and patience in answering a host of questions provided material which was unavailable elsewhere.

I would like also to express my gratitude to David R. Deener of Tulane University, under whose direction this study originally was undertaken as a Ph.D. thesis. Professor Deener's advice and assistance greatly improved the manuscript. In addition, I would like to acknowledge the valuable comments and suggestions of Professors John S. Gillespie, Henry L. Mason, Warren Roberts, Jr., and Robert S. Robins, all of Tulane University. A special word of thanks is extended to my wife, Dorothy, whose assistance and encouragement were invaluable throughout the preparation of this study.

INTRODUCTION

The peace time stationing for collective security purposes of large numbers of military personnel of one country in the territory of another country constitutes one of the most significant developments of postwar international relations. The United States, for example, has stationed nearly one half of its active military forces in over seventy countries since the Korean War broke out.[1] Stambuk noted that although the theories rationalizing this situation have changed, "the overseas bases and forces remain."[2] As a direct result of this stationing of large numbers of troops in foreign countries numerous bilateral and multilateral status of forces agreements have been put into force. One aspect of these agreements which has attracted considerable attention is the provisions dealing with the right to exercise criminal jurisdiction.[3]

As might be expected, a host of jurisdictional problems has arisen concerning whether jurisdictional rights lie with the states sending or the states receiving military personnel, the accompanying civilian component, and their dependents. As Snee and Pye have pointed out: "For the first time in the modern era, the sometimes radically different systems of law of two sovereign nations are operating within the same territory and in respect to the same individuals."[4] Thus a situation has arisen in which the relationships between the military authorities of the

[1] George Stambuk, *American Military Forces Abroad* (Columbus, Ohio: Ohio State University Press, 1963), pp. 3–4.

[2] *Ibid.*, p. 7. For a list of the collective security agreements to which the United States is a party and the countries involved, see *ibid.*, Appendix 1, pp. 185–189.

[3] As of 1956 the United States had unclassified agreements concerning jurisdiction over United States military personnel with forty-eight countries. For a list of these countries, see U.S., Congress, House, Committee on Foreign Affairs, *Hearings*, *Status of Forces Agreements*, 84th Cong., 2d Sess., 1956, Part 2, p. 159. See also U.S., Congress, Senate, Subcommittee of the Committee on Armed Services, *Hearings*, *Operation of Article VII, NATO Status of Forces Treaty*, 84th Cong., Ist Sess., 1955, p. 17; and Stambuk, Appendix 2, p. 190. Stambuk noted that the total number of agreements, including those classified, was sixty-five as of 1957. Stambuk, p. 48.

[4] Joseph M. Snee and Kenneth A. Pye, *Status of Forces Agreement* (New York: Oceana Publications, Inc., 1957), p. 10.

sending state and the civil authorities of the receiving state involve such matters as "the application of customs and duties, monetary exchange regulations, local taxation, motor vehicle laws, the settlement of claims and the impact of other local law, civil and criminal."[5] In these relationships a delicate balancing of interests must be established and maintained. On the one hand, if a military force in a foreign country is to fulfill its mission, it is necessary for that force to control its own personnel. On the other hand, "the territorial sovereign must have the power to protect its citizens and their property."[6] As Baldwin has noted, in a situation of this type

> the issues are of such complexity that a treaty or an agreement which defines precisely the status of the visiting force and specifies the respective powers which the receiving and sending states may properly exercise with regard to each other is absolutely essential.[7]

The best known and most studied of such arrangements are the criminal jurisdictional provisions of the North Atlantic Treaty Organization Status of Forces Agreement (NATO SOFA).[8] The provisions of the United States-Japanese agreement also have been dealt with in some detail.[9] In contrast, however, little attention has been given to the criminal jurisdictional arrangements of the numerous other agreements that are currently in force. This is true in spite of the fact that the pro-

[5] Gordon B. Baldwin, "Foreign Jurisdiction and the American Soldier: The Adventures of Girard," 1958 *Wisconsin Law Review* 52, 57 (1958).

Although the present study is concerned only with military forces, it should be pointed out that the matters mentioned above also become involved with respect to the personnel of international organizations, the governmental personnel connected with economic aid missions, and the personnel associated with such programs as the recently established United States Peace Corps program. The jurisdictional arrangements for the United States economic aid mission in the Philippines may be found in Article IV, paragraph 1 of the Economic and Technical Cooperation Agreement. Signed at Manila April 27, 1951; entered into force May 21, 1951. 3 *United States Treaties and Other International Agreements* [hereafter *UST*] 3707; *Treaties and Other International Acts Series* [hereafter *TIAS*] 2498. Under this agreement the personnel of the United States aid mission are considered to be a part "of the Diplomatic Mission of the United States... for the purpose of enjoying privileges and immunities..." The Peace Corps personnel have no such general immunity and with the exception of an exemption from various taxes and customs duties presumably have no more status than an United States visitor to the Philippines. The Philippine government, however, has agreed to "afford them, particularly in case of need, full aid and protection..." See Agreement Relating to the Establishment of a Peace Corps Program in the Republic of the Philippines. Exchange of notes signed at Manila October 11 and 31, 1961; entered into force October 31, 1961. 12 *UST* 1699; *TIAS* 4889.

[6] Bert A. Abrams, "International Law and Friendly Foreign Forces," 32 *New York University Law Review* 351, 355–356 (1957).

[7] Baldwin, p. 57.

[8] NATO SOFA. Signed at London June 19, 1951; entered into force for the United States August 23, 1953. 4 *UST* 1792; *TIAS* 2846.

[9] Agreement under Article VI of the Treaty of Mutual Cooperation and Security [11 *UST* 1632; *TIAS* 4509] Regarding Facilities and Areas and the Status of United States Armed Forces in Japan, with Agreed Minutes and Exchange of Notes. Signed at Washington January 19, 1960; entered into force June 23, 1960. 11 *UST* 1652; *TIAS* 4510.

visions of many of these agreements are substantially different from the NATO SOFA and the United States-Japanese agreement. If, as Snee and Pye have maintained, there is a new body of law developing with respect to jurisdiction under the status of forces agreements, it seems clear that students of international law will have to consider these "lesser" agreements as well as those that are more widely known.[10]

The present study is concerned with one such lesser-known agreement—that between the United States and the Philippines.[11] Originally the criminal jurisdictional arrangements for the United States forces in the Republic of the Philippines were included as Article XIII of the Military Bases Agreement of 1947. In August 1965, however, an agreement amending Article XIII was signed, putting into force criminal jurisdictional provisions which are significantly different from those of the original article.

Several articles by Filipino scholars and statesmen have dealt with the original arrangements included in the 1947 agreement. For the most part, however, these articles are incomplete and polemical in nature. A study by Meyer of the diplomatic history of the Philippines briefly mentions the criminal jurisdictional provisions as does a recent study by Taylor of Philippine-United States relations.[12] These works, like the Filipino articles, are sketchy and make no attempt to consider the jurisdictional arrangements in the context of international law. In addition, all of these studies are dated since they were written prior to the signing of the 1965 agreement. No study has been made pertaining to these new provisions.

The present study will examine in detail the criminal jurisdictional provisions of both the original Article XIII and those of the 1965 agree-

[10] Snee and Pye, p. 10.

[11] This study will be concerned only with the personnel of the United States military bases in the Philippines. It will not discuss the jurisdictional arrangements pertaining to the United States military advisory mission in the Philippines. In this mission the "senior officers enjoy full diplomatic immunites, while others are subject to the jurisdiction of Philippine courts to the extent that other members of our forces stationed therein are subject thereto..." U.S., Congress, Senate, Subcommittee of the Committee on Armed Services, *Hearings*, *Operation of Article VII, NATO Status of Forces Treaty*, 84th Cong., 2d Sess., 1956, p. 33. For the agreement, see Mutual Defense Assistance Agreement. Exchange of notes at Manila June 26, 1953; entered into force July 5, 1953. *TIAS* 2834. Nor will the jurisdictional arrangements under the Southeast Asia Treaty be discussed. There are no formal jurisdictional arrangements between all parties to this treaty. The United States, however, does have, in addition to the Philippine agreement, bilateral arrangements with Pakistan [see Annex B, Establishment of Communications Unit in Pakistan; signed at Karachi July 18, 1959; entered into force July 18, 1959; *TIAS* 4281] and Australia [see Article 8, Status of United States Forces in Australia; signed at Canberra May 9, 1963; entered into force May 9, 1963; *TIAS* 5349].

[12] Milton Walker Meyer, "A Diplomatic History of the Philippine Republic" (unpublished Ph.D. dissertation, Dept. of History, Stanford University, 1959); George E. Taylor, *The Philippines and the United States* (New York: Frederick A. Praeger, 1964).

ment. An attempt will be made to discuss systematically United States-Philippine relations with respect to the right to exercise criminal jurisdiction over United States military personnel, its accompanying civilian component, and their dependents, and, in certain classes of cases, the right to exercise jurisdiction over Filipinos. Where appropriate the jurisdictional provisions will be compared with those of other status of forces agreements.

Chapter I will supply necessary background material in the form of the pre-independence arrangements for the exercise of criminal jurisdiction relative to United States military and naval forces in the Philippines. The proposed post-independence status of United States military bases as provided for under the various United States congressional acts prior to independence together with a general review of the posture of the negotiations leading to the Military Bases Agreement of 1947 will be presented in Chapter II. The criminal jurisdictional provisions of the 1947 agreement will be set forth in Chapter III, while the various problems and cases which arose under these provisions will be discussed in Chapter IV. Chapter V will describe, mainly in terms of the attitudes of the two states, the progress made from 1954 to 1965 toward a revision of the criminal jurisdictional provisions of the 1947 agreement. [13] Chapter VI will discuss the criminal jurisdictional provisions of the 1965 agreement and the problems that are likely to arise under these provisions. It will then be possible to set forth in Chapter VII some general statements concerning the development of an international standard pertaining to the right to exercise criminal jurisdiction over friendly foreign armed forces.

It is hoped that this study because it specifically pertains to a status of forces agreement with an underdeveloped state will contribute to the knowledge of international law in the area that Snee and Pye refer to as "conjurisdictional law." Its primary interest, therefore, will be for the student of international law. Although little emphasis will be placed on United States-Philippine relations apart from the jurisdictional arrangements, there will be information included which will be of value to those concerned with the general relations between the two states. Finally, although no attempt will be made to discuss internal Filipino affairs, the study will be of interest to those concerned with the United States bases and their personnel as an issue in Philippine domestic politics.

[13] Most of the data required for a detailed study of the negotiations of both the 1947 agreement and the 1965 agreement are still classified. The intent of the present discussion is to set forth only the general posture of the situation between the United States and the Philippines as it affected the criminal jurisdictional arrangement.

CHAPTER I

CIVIL-MILITARY JURISDICTION WITH RESPECT TO UNITED STATES MILITARY FORCES IN THE PHILIPPINES 1898–1947

The criminal jurisdictional arrangements established between the Philippines and the United States after World War II were influenced by a background of practice that developed over the fifty years following American occupation of Manila in 1898.[1] This period afforded a variety of situations capable of generating conflicts of jurisdiction between civil and military authorities. These situations included war and insurrection, colonialism, and the peace time stationing in one independent nation of military forces of another independent nation. Under each of these diverse conditions some form of criminal jurisdictional arrangement was established.

War and Insurrection, 1898–1902

The period of war and insurrection in the Philippines began on May 1, 1898, when Commodore Perry destroyed the Spanish fleet in Manila Bay. Primarily due to the shortage of ground forces in the Philippine area, the United States did not attempt to occupy Manila until several months later. On August 12 an armistice was reached between the United States and Spain which granted the United States legal authority over Manila, and on August 13 the United States gained actual control over the city. At that time both the legal and actual authority of the United States were restricted to Manila. Spain retained legal sovereignty over all other areas of the Philippines until the exchange of the ratifications of the Treaty of Peace between Spain and the United States on April 11, 1899. The actual control of much of this area, however, was in the hands of the revolutionary forces of General Aguinaldo. These forces had been in revolt against the Spanish authorities prior to the outbreak of the Spanish-American War, and

[1] Conflicts of jurisdiction between the civil and military authorities under the Spanish regime in the Philippines fall outside the scope of this study; for treatment of these, see Emma Helen Blair and James Alexander Robertson (eds.), *The Philippine Islands 1493–1803*; beginning with Vol. 6, *The Philippine Islands 1493–1898* (55 vols.; Cleveland, Ohio: A. H. Clark Co., 1903–1909).

Aguinaldo had cooperated with the United States against Spain in hopes of gaining United States assistance in the establishment and maintenance of an independent Philippine Republic.[2] When it became clear that these hopes were in vain, Aguinaldo's cooperation ceased, and on February 4, 1899, fighting broke out between the United States and the insurgents. Thus when the United States gained legal sovereignty over all of the Philippines on April 11, the insurrection was in full operation.[3]

Upon occupying the city of Manila, Major General Merritt, commanding general of United States forces in the Philippines, established a military government,[4] a government which conformed to the general principles of international law pertaining to military occupation.[5] Under this government civil courts were suspended and military commissions and provost courts tried civilians for criminal offenses.[6]

[2] General Aguinaldo had proclaimed an independent Philippine Republic on June 12.

[3] For the history of this period, see Garel A. Grunder and William E. Livezey, *The Philippines and the United States* (Norman: University of Oklahoma Press, 1951), chaps. 1–4; John Foreman, *The Philippine Islands* (New York: Charles Scribner's Sons, 1899), chaps. 26 and 27; J. A. LeRoy, *The Americans in the Philippines* (2 vols.; Boston: Houghton, Mifflin Co., 1914), Vol. 1; Charles B. Elliott, *The Philippines to the End of the Military Regime* (Indianapolis: Bobbs-Merrill Co., 1916); James Henderson Blount, *The American Occupation of the Philippines* (New York: G. P. Putnam's Sons, 1912); and Leandro H. Fernandez, *The Philippine Republic* (New York: Columbia University, 1926).

[4] For the proclamation establishing the military government, dated August 14, 1898, see William Cameron Forbes, *The Philippine Islands* (Boston: Houghton, Mifflin Co., 1928), Vol. 2, Appendix 4, p. 429; and 24 *Official Opinions of the Attorneys-General of the United States* [hereafter *Op. A.G.*] 570, 573 (1903). See also *In re Calloway*, 1 Phil. 11 (1901); 1 [Philippine] *Official Gazette* [hereafter *Off. Gaz.*] 23–24 (1903); and *United States* v. *Tubig*, 3 Phil. 244 (1904). For "The powers, functions, and duties of the military government maintained by the United States in the islands lately ceded and relinquished by the Government of Spain," see Charles E. Magoon, *Reports on the Law of Civil Government in Territory Subject to Military Occupation by the Military Forces of the United States* (2d ed.; Washington: Government Printing Office, 1902), pp. 11–36. For the "Legal status of the territory and inhabitants of the islands acquired by the United States during the war with Spain, considered with reference to the territorial boundaries, the Constitution, and law of the United States," see *ibid.*, pp. 37–120.

[5] For the principles of international law pertaining to military occupation, see George B. Davis, *The Elements of International Law* (New York: Harper and Brothers Publishers, 1900), pp. 327–336; John Bassett Moore, *A Digest of International Law* (8 vols.; Washington: Government Printing Office, 1906), Vol. 7, pp. 257–315; Percy Bordwell. *The Law of War Between Belligerents* (Chicago: Callaghan and Co., 1908), chap. 8; Charles H. Stockton, *Outlines of International Law* (New York: Charles Scribner's Sons, 1914), pp. 364–379; Charles G. Fenwick, *International Law* (2d ed. rev.; New York: D. Appleton-Century Co., 1934), pp. 485–491; Gerhard von Glahn, *The Occupation of Enemy Territory* (Minneapolis: University of Minnesota Press, 1957); and William W. Bishop, Jr., *International Law* (2d ed. rev.; Boston: Little, Brown and Co., 1962), pp. 815–837.

[6] See 24 *Op. A.G.* 570, 571 (1903). For summaries of such trials, see Department of the Pacific, "Report of Headquarters Pacific and Eighth Army Corps, Office of Judge Advocate," *Report of the Major General Commanding the Army* in *Annual Reports of the War Department for the Fiscal Year Ended June 30, 1899* [hereafter *War Department 1899*] (U.S., Congress, House Document No. 2, 56th Cong., 1st Sess., 1899–1900), Vol. 5, Part 2, pp. 181–187; U.S., Congress, Senate Document No. 205 (*Charges of Cruelty, Etc., to the Natives of the Philippines*), in *Senate Documents* (57th Cong., 1st Sess., 1901–1902), Vol. 15; War Department, *Reports of*

Gradually, however, the civil courts were restored and resumed their former jurisdiction with respect to civilians, first in civil and then in criminal cases. This restoration was begun by the military government and continued by the Philippine Commission, a commission established in September 1900 by executive order of the President and directed "to continue and perfect the work of organizing and establishing civil government already commenced by the military authorities."[7]

With respect to military personnel, however, these civil courts had no jurisdiction. By orders of instruction of August 22, 1898, the general in command provided that the local courts had no right to exercise jurisdiction over crimes committed by military personnel.[8] These orders were in effect throughout the Islands even in those areas completely pacified, under the control of the Philippine Commission rather than the military, and with a complete system of civil courts.

Following the United States Supreme Court in *Coleman* v. *Tennessee*[9] and *Dow* v. *Johnson*,[10] the United States-established Philippine Supreme Court[11] consistently held that the military tribunals had exclusive

he Secretary of War, Chief of Staff, Adjutant General, Inspector General, and Judge-Advocate-General, n *War Department 1903* (U.S., Congress, House Document No. 2, 58th Cong., 2d Sess., 1903–1904), Vol. 1, p. 477.

[7] As cited in Forbes, Vol. 2, Appendix 7, p. 439. For the re-establishment of the civil court system, see War Department, "Report for 1900," *Annual Reports of the Secretary of War, 1899–1903* (Washington: Government Printing Office, 1904), pp. 99–100; War Department, "Report for 1901," *ibid.*, pp. 206–207; "Report of the Chief Justice of the [Philippines] Supreme Court to the U.S. Military Governor," *Report of The Military Governor of the Philippine Islands on Civil Affairs*, in *War Department 1900* (U.S., Congress, House Documents No. 2, 56th Cong., 2d Sess., 1900–1901), Vol. 1, Part 10, Appendix GG, pp. 154–161; *Report of the Philippine Commission*, in *War Department 1901* (U.S., Congress, House Document No. 2, 57th Cong., 1st Sess., 1901–1902), Vol. 7, Part 1, pp. 73–91; "Report of the Secretary of Finance and Justice," *Report of the Philippine Commission*, in *War Department 1902* (U.S., Congress, House Document No. 2, 57th Cong., 2d Sess., 1902–1903), Vol. 10, Part 2, pp. 691–697; *Report of the Philippine Commission*, in *War Department 1903* (U.S., Congress, House Document No. 2, 58th Cong., 2d Sess., 1903–1904), Vol. 7, Part 3. For Philippine acts re-establishing the civil courts, see *Public Laws and Resolutions Passed by the Philippine Commission*, in *War Department 1901* (Washington: Government Printing Office, 1901), Vol. 1, Part 10 [Act No. 136 (June 11, 1901), pp. 289–306; Act. No. 186 (August 5, 1901), pp. 422–423; Act No. 190 (September 1, 1901), pp. 425–581]; and *Acts of the Philippine Commission*, in *War Department 1902* (U.S., Congress, House Document No. 2, 57th Cong., 2d Sess., 1902–1903), Vol. 11 [Act No. 272 (October 21, 1901), p. 36; Act No. 400 (May 16, 1902), pp. 340–341; Act No. 421 (June 23, 1902), pp. 361–362]. See also Forbes, Vol. 1, pp. 294–295.

[8] See 24 *Op. A.G.* 570, 573 (1903).

[9] *Coleman* v. *Tennessee*, 97 U.S. 509 (1878).

[10] *Dow* v. *Johnson*, 100 U.S. 148 (1879).

[11] According to the 1900 annual report of the Secretary of War, the military authorities "promptly commenced the organization of civil administration, in which, as rapidly as practicable, all the ordinary functions of government were to be vested." The first step in the applications of the "excellent and adequate" substantive body of Spanish law was to organize the courts. Thus the military authorities set up a ten-man Supreme Court, composed of seven Filipinos and three United States officers. This court was supplemented by subordinate courts, first for the city of Manila and then for other regions as the occupation was extended. See "Report for 1900," *Annual Reports of the Secretary of War, 1899–1903*, pp. 99–100. The

jurisdiction to try and to punish offenses of military personnel until the official ending of the insurrection.[12] The same view was taken by Attorney General Knox in an advisory opinion requested by Secretary of War Root. Attorney General Knox pointed out that *Coleman* v. *Tennessee*

> held that when the armies of the United States were in the enemy's country the established military tribunals had, under the laws of war and statutory authority, exclusive jurisdiction to try and to punish offenses of every grade committed by persons in the military service.

Knox further maintained, as did the Philippine Supreme Court, that this applied to the insurrection in the Philippines.[13]

In addition to the problems which were produced by conflicts of jurisdiction between the civil and military authorities during the insurrection, difficulties also arose due to United States constitutional practice which placed a certain class of cases outside the jurisdiction of both civil and military authorities. Because of this lacuna no action could be taken, for example, in the Brownell case, which involved an offense committed by a United States Army captain in the Philippines in 1900. Under the captain's orders, a priest was tortured; shortly

court system was later stabilized on three levels: the Supreme Court; Courts of First Instance; and justice of the peace courts. From the time of the Organic Act of 1902 until the establishment of the Philippine Commonwealth in 1935, the Supreme Court justices were appointed by the President of the United States with the consent of the United States Senate. The judges of the Courts of First Instance and the justices of the peace were appointed by the Governor General, at first with the consent of the Philippine Commission and later with the consent of the Philippine Senate. After the establishment of the Commonwealth all judicial appointments were made by the President of the Philippines with the consent of the Commission on Appointments of the Philippine legislature. "From the beginning of the American regime until shortly after its end in 1935 both Americans and Filipinos served on the Supreme Court and the courts of first instance. Save in a few special jurisdictions all of the justices of the peace were Filipinos. From the beginning the Chief Justice was invariably a Filipino; but except during the brief existence of the Supreme Court established by the military governor and a few months before the inauguration of the Commonwealth, an American majority was maintained on the Supreme Court. In 1902 there were ten American and six Filipino judges of first instance." The percentage of Americans increased until 1904 but from that time on the percentage of Americans decreased. By 1926 only two of the fifty-three judges of first instance were Americans. Joseph Ralston Hayden, *The Philippines* (New York: Macmillan Co., 1942), p. 243. In 1919 a noted Filipino scholar, Professor Maximo M. Kalaw, stated that although the majority of the Supreme Court justices were Americans, its personnel was not a "political factor." He stated that the Supreme Court had "fitly held itself aloof from purely political controversies, and has gained the popular respect and reverence it justly deserves." Kalaw, *Self-Government in the Philippines* (New York: The Century Co., 1919), p. 39. For the court system during the colonial period, see Hayden, chap. 10; Forbes, Vol. 1, chap. 7; and Dean C. Worcester, *The Philippines Past and Present* (New edition in one volume with biographical sketch and four additional chapters by Joseph Hayden; New York: Macmillan Co., 1930), chap. 15.

12 See *United States* v. *Colley*, 3 Phil. 58 (1903); and *United States* v. *Tubig*, 3 Phil. 244 (1904).

13 24 *Op.A.G.* 570, 571–572, 574 (1903). See also Department of the Navy, *Laws Relating to the Navy, Annotated* (Washington: Government Printing Office, 1922), p. 1001.

thereafter the priest died. In an advisory opinion of 1903 the Attorney General of the United States stated that the accused was subject to neither the jurisdiction of the military nor the civil authorities: (1) because the accused had left the service and was no longer subject to court-martial jurisdiction; (2) because a military commission no longer had jurisdiction since peace had been proclaimed in the Philippines; and (3) because during a period of war the civil courts had no jurisdiction over military personnel in a combat zone.[14]

The Territorial Period, 1902–1935

The situation with respect to jurisdiction over the military changed with the passage by Congress of the First Organic Act of July 1, 1902,[15] and the official ending of the insurrection by presidential proclamation on July 4, 1902.[16] With the end of the insurrection also came the end of the jurisdictional arrangement that prevailed previously. By the provisions of the Organic Act, as the United States Solicitor General later pointed out, Congress did not distinguish "between crimes committed by or against military persons or between crimes so committed on or off a military reservation." He further noted that since Congress

> has exclusive jurisdiction everywhere in a Territory, and has made no exception regarding a military reservation, it would seem that Congress intends the jurisdiction over ordinary crimes to be exercised by the local courts.[17]

The latter is premised on the view of the United States Supreme Court in *Coleman* v. *Tennessee* which stated:

> With the known hostility of the American people to any interference by the military with the regular administration of justice in the civil courts, no such intention (to confer exclusive jurisdiction upon a court-martial) should be ascribed to Congress in the absence of clear and direct language to that effect.[18]

As Attorney General Wickersham pointed out in an advisory opinion of

[14] See 24 *Op.A.G.* 570, 570–574 (1903). A similar case arose in Mexico during the Mexican War. In that case, as in the Brownell case, the Attorney General ruled that the alleged offender was not subject to the jurisdiction of either the civil or military courts. See 5 *Op.A.G.* 55 (1848). For further comment on this jurisdictional difficulty, see below, this chap., p. 13, and note 49.

[15] 32 *Statutes at Large* [hereafter *Stat.*] 691 (1902).

[16] For the proclamation of President Roosevelt, see "Report for 1902," *Annual Reports of the Secretary of War, 1899–1903*, Appendix C, pp. 465–466.

[17] Solicitor General, for Defendant in Error, *Grafton* v. *United States*, 206 U.S. 333, 338 (1907).

[18] *Coleman* v. *Tennessee*, 97 U.S. 509, 514 (1878), as quoted in 28 *Op.A.G.* 24, 25 (1909).

1909, the general rule "is that the jurisdiction of civil courts is concurrent as to offenses triable before courts-martial."[19]

Under this construction there would be concurrent jurisdiction in the Philippines by civil and military authorities in cases involving military personnel. This, in fact, was the point of view taken by the Supreme Court of the United States when, on appeal from the Philippine Supreme Court, *Grafton* v. *United States* was decided in 1907.[20] The decision held that the civil courts and the military courts in the Philippines were created by the same sovereign, and thus the two court systems had concurrent jurisdiction in criminal cases involving military personnel. Therefore, the Court held that Grafton, a private in the United States Army, was subject to the jurisdiction of either the civil or the military courts, even though his alleged offense occurred within a military reservation and during a period when he was on duty as a sentry.[21] The Court decided that

> while... the jurisdiction of general courts-martial extends to all crimes, not capital, committed against public law by an officer or soldier of the Army within the limits of the territory in which he is serving, this jurisdiction is not exclusive, but only concurrent with that of the civil courts.[22]

The Court stated that the question of which court—civil or military—would exercise jurisdiction would be determined by which obtained jurisdiction first. It was further noted that

> any possible conflict in these matters, between civil and military courts, can be obviated either by withholding from courts-martial all authority to try officers or soldiers for crimes prescribed by the civil power, leaving the civil tribunals to try such offenses, or by investing courts-martial with exclusive jurisdiction to try such officers and soldiers for all crimes, not capital.[23]

By so stating the Court indicated that the elimination of conflicts of jurisdiction was a legislative matter.

[19] 28 *Op.A.G.* 24, 25 (1909), citing 6 *Op.A.G.* 413 (1854).

[20] *Grafton* v. *United States*, 206 U.S. 333 (1907), on appeal from *United States* v. *Grafton*, 6 Phil. 55 (1906).

[21] Earlier, it should be noted, the Philippine Commission had asserted jurisdiction over the military reservations with its passage of Act No. 530 on November 24, 1902. For purposes of this study the central provision of Act No. 530 was that of Section 8. This section stated: "All laws or parts of laws in force in the Philippine Islands not inconsistent with military use of any public land reserved by the President for military purposes shall be in full force and effect over said lands." *Acts of the Philippine Commission*, in *War Department 1903* (U.S., Congress, House Document No. 2, 58th Cong., 2d Sess., 1903–1904), Vol. 8, pp. 230–231.

[22] *Grafton* v. *United States*, 206 U.S. 333, 348 (1907). "A general court-martial has, under existing statutes, in time of peace, jurisdiction to try an officer or soldier of the Army for any offense, not capital, which the civil law declares to be a crime against the public." *Ibid.* p. 351.

[23] *Ibid.*, pp. 350, 352–353.

Thus in the *Grafton* case the United States Supreme Court clearly held that there was concurrent jurisdiction with respect to military personnel for both on- and off-base offenses. This, however, was not the case with respect to jurisdiction over civilian offenders, either on or off the bases. After the amnesty proclamation and the passage of the Organic Act, civilians committing off-base offenses were subject to civil law only. Considerable confusion existed, however, concerning the question of jurisdiction over a civilian who had committed an offense on a military base.[24] This confusion was due to the difficulty in interpreting both section 12 of the Organic Act of 1902 and the presidential orders designating military reservations in the Philippines.

Section 12 of the Organic Act provided:

> That all property and rights which may have been acquired in the Philippine Islands by the United States under the treaty of peace with Spain, signed December tenth, eighteen hundred and ninety-eight, *except such land or other property as shall be designated by the President of the United States for military and other reservations of the Government of the United States*, are hereby placed under the control of the government of said islands to be administered for the benefit of the inhabitants thereof, except as provided in this Act.[25]

It was under the authority of this provision that the President reserved for naval and military purposes certain land in the Philippines. Typical of the executive orders setting aside land for military and naval reservations was the order pertaining to the Subic Bay reservation. This order stated that certain land was "'reserved for naval purposes, and said reservation and all lands included within such boundaries' were 'placed under the governance and control of the Navy Department.'"[26] The United States Attorney General was asked to interpret this order as to whether or not it was authorization for the Navy to set up a municipal government on the reservation. He stated that the "real question" was:

> Which branch of the Federal authority, the Philippine government or the Navy Department, shall exercise the municipal jurisdiction claimed, both executive and

[24] This confusion was in part due to the large number of Filipinos living within the reservations set aside for military and naval purposes. Because of the refusal of high-level planners to come to a definite position on which bases were to be developed, no decision was made as to the disposition of civilians or their property within the reservations. See *Report of the Philippine Division*, in *War Department 1909* (Washington: Government Printing Office, 1910), Vol. 3, p. 173; and *Report of the Philippine Division*, in *War Department 1910* (Washington: Government Printing Office, 1910), Vol. 3, p. 189. A case in point is Olongapo, a city of some 60,000 inhabitants, which until 1959 was included within Subic Bay Naval Base.

[25] 32 *Stat.* 691, 695 (1902). Emphasis added. The Jones Act of August 29, 1916, reiterates this provision. 39 *Stat.* 545, 547 (1916).

[26] As cited in 26 *Op.A.G.* 91 (1906).

judicial, on the reservation, over property, not owned by the United States and persons not in its military service.[27]

The Attorney General pointed out that section 12 of the Organic Act "simply grants and reserves property; it does not confer governmental jurisdiction. It deals with property belonging to the government, but does not grant the power to exercise the functions of government."[28] He further stated that the intention of the executive order of the President was "to commit to the particular Department the administration of the property for public use, without contemplating any separate establishment of municipal government." He added that military necessity did not require absolute naval control.[29] Earlier the Attorney General of the Philippine Islands had stated:

It is... my opinion that, in accordance with said [Organic] Act of Congress, the general laws enacted by the Philippine Commission have force and effect throughout the Philippine Islands unless hereafter limited in their operation by act of Congress, or unless portions of the territory of the Philippine Islands be withdrawn by Congress from the territorial jurisdiction of the Philippine Commission.[30]

Notwithstanding these opinions and the sources cited therein, the Navy in 1920 did establish what amounted to a civil government at Subic Bay, Olongapo, Zambales Province. According to the "Laws and Regulations for the Organization and Administration of the United States Naval Reservation, Olongapo, Philippine Islands," the reservation police judge had original jurisdiction over violations of the "Laws and Regulations" with respect to civilians on the reservation, and could administer fines and punishments "as might be imposed by a justice of the peace in a civil community for like offenses under the Penal Code of the Philippine Islands." In cases beyond the jurisdiction of a civil justice of the peace the police judge was "directed to turn the accused over to the local [civil] justice of the peace, to be bound over to the Court of First Instance of Zambales [Province]."[31]

[27] *Ibid.*, p. 95.

[28] *Ibid.*, p. 98.

[29] *Ibid.*, p. 93. Following a discussion of the language of other executive orders establishing reservations and the interpretation of such language, the Attorney General stated: "The military control up to the limit of military necessities would be paramount; but such a charter of government as is deduced here [by the Navy Department] from the President's language has not been attached to any other order of military reservation, although couched in similar terms.

"The conclusion, then, is natural that the intention of the President's language ['governance and control'] was as usual [in other orders establishing military reservations], to commit to the particular Department the administration of the property for the public use, without contemplating any separate establishment of municipal government." *Ibid.*

[30] 1 *Official Opinions of the Attorney-General of the Philippine Islands* 326, 334–335 (1903). See also *ibid.*, pp. 329–330.

[31] *Payomo* v. *Floyd*, 42 Phil. 788, 790–791, 800 (1922).

Two years after the establishment of this government, however, the Philippine Supreme Court in the *Payomo* case adopted the previously cited opinions of both the United States and the Philippine Attorneys General regarding the status of civilians on the bases. The *Payomo* case involved Claixto Mendigorin, a Filipino civilian resident of Subic, Zambales, who was arrested by the naval authorities for cutting timber on the reservation without a permit and was sentenced by the naval reservation police judge. In a petition for a writ of habeas corpus, filed on Mendigorin's behalf by Payomo, the Philippine Supreme Court held that the civil courts of the Philippines had jurisdiction over petitions for habeas corpus filed by civilians detained by naval authorities. The Court went on to say that the Navy Department "had no authority to make laws binding on the civil population" and "no power to set up a court, or office, in the Olongapo Reservation with jurisdiction over matters cognizable under the penal laws of the Philippine Islands..."[32] The Court agreed that "military control [on the bases] up to the point of necessity [was] paramount," but maintained that military control did not necessitate "the exercise of the functions of government over the civilian population of the reservation."[33] Mendigorin, therefore, was ordered released for want of jurisdiction.

Thus the *Payomo* case and the earlier *Grafton* case set forth the arrangements which existed after the end of the insurrection in 1902. According to the *Payomo* case the military authorities did not have the right to exercise jurisdiction over civilian offenders for offenses committed on the bases. According to the *Grafton* case there was concurrent jurisdiction over all offenses by military personnel which were violations of both civil and military law. No distinction was made as to whether the offense occurred on or off base or whether the offender was on or off duty.

The United States High Commissioner to the Philippines later reported that the existence of concurrent jursidiction over military personnel resulted in "considerable trouble and bickering between the civil authorities and the Army and Navy high commands in the Philippines."[34] In an effort to clarify the situation the Governor General in 1912 issued Executive Order Number 50. In brief, the order: (1) di-

[32] *Ibid.*, p. 794.

[33] *Ibid.*, p. 796. Olongapo, within the Subic Bay Reservation, had a civilian population of just under 10,000 at this time.

[34] United States High Commissioner to the Philippines, *Third Annual Report of the United States High Commissioner to the Philippine Islands to the President and Congress of the United States Covering the Calender Year 1938 and the First Six Months of 1939* (Washington: Government Printing Office, 1943) [hereafter, High Commissioner, *Third Annual Report*], p. 13.

rected civil officials to turn over all army personnel accused of minor offenses to the military authorities for courts-martial proceedings; (2) directed civil officials to try accused army personnel in civil courts in cases involving offenses punishable by more than one year imprisonment; and (3) provided that army personnel accused of offenses be placed in the custody of military authorities during pretrial and trial proceedings.[35] Not only did this executive order clarify the situation, but also it increased military jurisdiction over certain classes of cases involving military personnel.

According to the Philippine High Commissioner's report for 1938-1939, this jurisdictional arrangement worked well until large numbers of auto accidents involving military personnel and civilians began to occur. This situation precipitated friction between civil and military authorities in their efforts to obtain jurisdiction over military offenders, primarily because in the Philippines "criminal and civil issues are tried together, and the award of civil damages, if any, is made at the same time that sentence is passed."[36]

The Commonwealth Period, 1935–1942

The jurisdictional arrangements set forth in Executive Order Number 50 apparently remained unchanged into the Commonwealth period.[37] It was not until May 1938 that Executive Order Number 151, which had been initiated by High Commissioner McNutt, was approved by the Commonwealth authorities.[38] The chief provisions of the

[35] For the text of Executive Order No. 50, effective September 12, 1912, see 10 *Off. Gaz.* 1607 (1912); and High Commissioner, *Third Annual Report*, pp. 13–14. In 1929 the order was amended to include naval personnel. *Ibid.*, p. 14.

[36] *Ibid.* General Order 58, the original basic criminal law set forth by the United States, provided that the injured party in a criminal offense could participate in the case and "the court upon conviction of the accused may enter judgment against him for the damages occasioned by his wrongful act," thus leaving in the Philippine law the Spanish provision for the trial of a civil and criminal action at the same time. See "General Order No. 58, Office of the United States Military Governor in the Philippine Islands, April 23, 1900, as amended by Acts of the Philippine Commission to September 1, 1908," *Acts of First Philippine Legislature*, in *War Department 1908* (Washington: Government Printing Office, 1908), Vol. 9, pp. 163–174.

[37] While the Philippine Independence [Tydings-McDuffie] Act [48 *Stat.* 456 (1934)] was under consideration by Congress in 1934, the "Commanding General, Philippine Department [United States Army], recommended to the Secretary of War that provision be made in the act for criminal jurisdiction over service personnel to be vested in the Army and Navy authorities. The recommendation did not prosper." High Commissioner, *Third Annual Report*, p. 14.

[38] Eight months earlier, Manuel Quezon, as Commonwealth president, had issued Administrative Order No. 43 [35 *Off. Gaz.* 1903 (1937)], which in some respects increased the role of the civil authorities in handling offenses involving military personnel. The difference between Administrative Order No. 43 and Executive Order No. 50, however, was

order, as summarized in the report of the High Commissioner, were as follows:

a. It gives the military and naval authorities jurisdiction in all criminal cases involving service personnel except a few common law crimes (homicide, rape, larceny, etc.).

b. It gives the military and naval authorities exclusive jurisdiction over crimes involving military and naval personnel which are committed on military or naval reservations.

c. It gives the military and naval authorities exclusive jurisdiction over crimes involving military and naval personnel, when such persons are engaged in the performance of duties.

d. It reserves the rights of civilians to bring civil actions for damages against military and naval personnel in the local courts.[39]

Executive Order Number 151 was a radical departure not only from the jurisdictional arrangements established under Executive Order Number 50 but also from the civil-military jurisdictional arrangements within the continental limits of the United States. As has been noted, "undoubtedly the general rule is that [in peace time] the jurisdiction of civil courts is concurrent as to offenses triable before courts-martial."[40] While Executive Order Number 50 departed only slightly from this rule, Executive Order Number 151 placed important limitations on the types of offenses which were subject to concurrent jurisdiction.[41] In spite of this, at least according to McNutt's report of 1938–1939, the order was "a satisfactory and equitable solution to the problem," and it was working "well."[42] Apparently this order continued in effect until the Japanese invaded the Philippines in 1941.

The Japanese Occupation, 1942–1945

Court decisions after the war held that the Japanese occupation of

slight. In spite of its minor importance High Commissioner McNutt apparently thought this was a step in the wrong direction. According to his report, he "questioned" the new order, stating that he did not believe it was acceptable. After "discussions" between McNutt and Quezon, a new executive order, having been prepared by the legal section of McNutt's office, in conjunction with the Staff Judge Advocate, Philippine Department, was submitted to the Commonwealth authorities and approved. Certainly it is not improbable that McNutt was planning to change the jurisdictional arrangement before the dispute over Quezon's administrative order arose. See High Commissioner, *Third Annual Report*, pp. 14–15.

[39] *Ibid.*, p. 15. For the text of Executive Order No. 151, see 36 *Off. Gaz.* 1527 (1938).

[40] U.S. Department of the Navy, *Laws Relating to the Navy, Annotated* (Washington: Government Printing Office, 1922), pp. 66, 120, citing *Franklin* v. *United States*, 216 U.S. 559, 568 (1910); *United States* v. *Clark*, 31 Fed. Rep. 710 (1887); and 6 *Op.A.G.* 413, 419 (1854).

[41] Hayden stated that High Commissioner McNutt "vigorously" vindicated "certain American rights which had been called into question." Hayden, pp. 781–782. With respect to jurisdiction over United States military and naval personnel, however, McNutt, by gaining approval of Executive Order No. 151, did more than "vindicate" American rights he radically extended them.

[42] High Commissioner, *Third Annual Report*, p. 15.

the Philippines began on January 2, 1942, and ended on February 3, 1945.[43] At the beginning of the occupation the Japanese established a military administration under martial law and extended "courts-martial jurisdiction for certain actions over the inhabitants of the Islands."[44] Later the Philippine Executive Commission, an executive organ of the Japanese military administration, set up other courts for the handling of civilian cases. Although these courts "exercised a general jurisdiction over inhabitants of the Islands," as Cho has noted, they did not entirely eliminate courts-martial jurisdiction over civilians.[45] Moreover, the civilian courts had no jurisdiction over members of the Japanese occupation forces, as these forces were "subject only to the jurisdiction of Japanese courts-martial."[46] Thus the jurisdictional arrangements which prevailed during the Japanese occupation were comparable to those which the United States had implemented during the insurrection at the turn of the century.

After the war the Philippine courts consistently held that the decisions handed down by the courts during the occupation period were considered to be valid and subsisting so long as the Japanese were in control, and of continuing force after the occupation provided that the offense for which the sentence was imposed was not a political offense or provided that the offense was not directed against the public generally but primarily against the Japanese occupation force.[47]

[43] See Claro M. Recto, *The Law of Belligerent Occupation with Particular Reference to the Japanese Occupation of the Philippines and the Effect of the Change of Sovereignty on the Commonwealth Treason Law* (Manila: People's Publishers, 1946); and Recto, *Three Years of Enemy Occupation* (Manila: People's Publishers, 1946), as cited in Sung Yoon Cho, "Jurisdiction over Foreign Forces in Japan, 1945–1960" (unpublished Ph.D. dissertation, Dept. of Political Science, Tulane University, 1964), p. 19.

[44] *Ibid.*, citing Proclamation of January 2, 1942, and Proclamation of January 3, 1942, *The Official Journal of the Japanese Military Occupation*, Number 1 (1942), pp. 1–2.

[45] Cho, "Jurisdiction over Foreign Forces in Japan, 1945–1960," p. 20. Examples of acts prescribed for courts-martial jurisdiction were: "Any person who rebels against the Japanese forces; any person who intentionally or falsely guides the Japanese forces, warships or transports; any person who kills or inflicts injuries upon an Imperial Japanese soldier, civilian employees of the Army and Navy or hinders the execution of the duties of the above-mentioned persons; and any person who refuses to obey any orders of military necessity issued by the Japanese Forces." *Ibid.*, note 44.

[46] *Ibid.*, p. 21, citing Recto, *The Law of Belligerent Occupation...*

[47] See *Peralta* v. *Director of Prisons*, 75 Phil. 285 (1945); *Co Kim Cham* v. *Tan Keh*, 75 Phil. 371 (1945); *Herrero* v. *Dias*, 75 Phil. 489 (1945); *Alcantara* v. *Director of Prisons*, 75 Phil. 494 (1945); *People* v. *Jose*, 75 Phil. 612 (1945); *Asican* v. *Quirino*, 75 Phil. 791 (1946); *Haw Pia* v. *China Banking Corporation*, 80 Phil. 604 (1948); *Pastrana* v. *Director of Prisons*, 84 Phil. 357 (1949); *People* v. *Tuason*, 84 Phil. 670 (1949); *Tan Tuan* v. *Lucena Food Control Board*, 84 Phil. 687 (1949); *Estate of McDonough* v. *Philippine National Bank*, 88 Phil. 625 (1951); *Suller* v. *Perez*, 92 Phil. 216 (1952). See also L. D. Lockwood, "The Philippine Supreme Court and Postwar Problems of International Law," 3 *Stanford Law Review* 3 (1950). This does not mean, however, that no steps were taken against Japanese military officials for their actions in the

It should be noted that a case arose in 1947 which involved an offense committed during the Japanese occupation. This case, which was similar to the earlier Brownell case, involved an offense over which there was a lack of jurisdiction by either the civil or military authorities. As summarized by Deener, the facts of this case were as follows:

> Hirshberg, taken prisoner by the Japanese in the Philippines, was liberated [in September 1945], hospitalized and restored to duty by the Navy [in January 1946]. Later he was granted an honorable discharge, but re-enlisted immediately. During... [this] enlistment he was convicted by a general court-martial of maltreatment of fellow prisoners during his internment by the Japanese.[49]

This conviction later was overturned by a United States Supreme Court decision which held that a court-martial had no jurisdiction to try an enlisted man for offenses committed during a prior enlistment terminated by an honorable discharge, even though he re-enlisted immediately.[49]

United States Reoccupation and the Postwar Period

When the United States reoccupied the Philippines in late 1944 and early 1945 and re-established the Commonwealth, the prewar jurisdictional arrangements were not automatically resumed. During the period from the reoccupation to the signing of the Military Bases Agreement in March 1947, which included the granting of Philippine independence on July 4, 1946, the United States military authorities

Philippines during the occupation. Some, in fact, were tried for violations of the laws of war, and the right to do so was upheld by the Philippine Supreme Court. See, in particular, *Yamashita* v. *Styler*, 75 Phil. 563 (1945), upheld at *In re Yamashita*, 327 U.S. 1 (1946).

[48] David R. Deener, *The United States Attorneys General and International Law* (The Hague: Martinus Nijhoff, 1957), p. 237, note 9.

[49] *Hirshberg* v. *Cooke*, 336 U.S. 210 (1949). Apparently in an effort to eliminate the United States constitutional practice which led to this jurisdictional lacuna, Congress, in 1950, included in the Uniform Code of Military Justice (UCMJ) a provision which stated that "any person charged with having committed, while in a status in which he was subject to this code, an offense against this code, punishable by confinement of five years or more and for which the person cannot be tried in the courts of the United States or any State or Territory thereof or of the District of Columbia, shall not be relieved from amenability to trial by courts-martial by reason of the termination of said status." Article 3(a), UCMJ, 64 *Stat.* 107 (1950). This provision later was declared unconstitutional by the Supreme Court in *United States ex rel. Toth* v. *Quarles*, 350 U.S. 11 (1955), mainly on the grounds that the constitutional grant of power to Congress to regulate the armed forces did not empower Congress to deprive civilians of trials under the safeguards of the Bill of Rights. Thus, this jurisdictional lacuna has continued. The Court noted in the *Toth* case, however, that it would have been constitutionally justified for Congress to confer jurisdiction on federal district courts to try any person for an offense violating the UCMJ if he were no longer subject to military jurisdiction. Thus, as the Court stated, "there can be no valid argument that civilian ex-servicemen must be tried by court-martial or not at all. If that is so it is only because Congress has not seen fit to subject them to trial in federal district courts." *Ibid.*, pp. 20–21.

exercised exclusive jurisdiction over their military personnel. This arrangement was based on two decisions by the Philippine Supreme Court, one in *Raquiza* v. *Bradford* and the other in the *Tubb* case.[50]

Raquiza v. *Bradford* was an original action before the Court in which three civilian women interned by the United States military authorities under the provisions of a proclamation by General MacArthur, dated December 29, 1944, petitioned for a writ of habeas corpus.[51] The Court denied the petition, applying the "well-settled principle" of international law that a friendly foreign army allowed to march through or to be stationed in a friendly country by permission is exempt from the civil and criminal jurisdiction of the place. Citing *Coleman* v. *Tennessee*, the Court maintained:

> If a foreign army permitted to be stationed in a friendly country 'by permission of its government or sovereign' is exempt from the civil and criminal jurisdiction of the place, with much more reason should the Army of the United States, which is not only permitted by the Commonwealth Government to be stationed here but... [is in the Philippines for the purpose of liberating the Philippines and prosecuting the war to a successful conclusion], be exempt from the civil and criminal jurisdiction of the place, at least for the time covered by said agreement of the two Governments.[52] By analogy [with *Coleman* v. *Tennessee*] an attempt of our civil courts to exercise jurisdiction over the United States Army before such period expires, would be considered as a violation of this country's faith... [The] agreement for the stationing of the United States Army or a part of its forces in the Philippines implies a waiver of all jurisdiction over their troops during the time covered by such agreement, and permits the allied general or commander in chief to retain that exclusive control and discipline which the government of his army may require.[53]

Thus the six-man majority held that the friendly and foreign United States Army was beyond the jurisdiction of the Philippines courts.

There were, however, certain aspects of the Court's reasoning in

[50] *Raquiza* v. *Bradford*, 75 Phil. 50 (1945); *Tubb and Tedrow* v. *Griess*, 78 Phil. 249 (1947).

[51] For the text of MacArthur's proclamation, see 41 *Off. Gaz.* 148 (1945). In the *Raquiza* case the Court noted that General MacArthur's proclamation was premised upon "two grave reasons": "(1) that evidence was before him 'that certain citizens of the Philippines voluntarily have given aid, comfort and sustenance to the enemy in violation of allegiance due to the Governments of the United States and the Commonwealth of the Philippines'; and (2) that 'military necessity requires that such persons be removed from any opportunity to threaten the security of our military forces or the success of our military operation.'" The purpose of the proclamation was to provide a basis for holding in restraint those persons referred to, "when apprehended, 'for the duration of the war; whereafter I shall release them to the Philippine Government for its judgment upon their respective cases.'" *Raquiza* v. *Bradford*, 75 Phil. 50, 57 (1945). Under the provisions of MacArthur's proclamation a large number of Filipinos were apprehended and held in custody by the United States military authorities, among them the petitioners in the *Raquiza* case.

[52] Author's note. An agreement was concluded between Presidents Truman and Osmeña in May 1945 which provided for the continuation of the United States bases in the Philippines. See below, p. 25.

[53] *Raquiza* v. *Bradford*, 75 Phil. 50, 61 (1945).

reaching this decision that were questioned in the dissent of Justice Ozaeta.[54] Justice Ozaeta noted that "the United States Army is not foreign to the Philippines." It is here "by right of sovereignty of the United States over the Philippines," and not "by permission or invitation of the Philippine Government." Therefore, Justice Ozaeta maintained that the United States Army had the same right to be in the Philippines as it had to be in Hawaii or California. He continued by stating:

> The case at bar is not like the *Coleman* case wherein a member of the United States Army of occupation was indicted by the enemy state for a crime committed against a citizen of the latter after he had been tried and convicted by a proper court-martial. This is a case wherein nationals of the United States living under the protection of the United States are being deprived of their liberty by members of that Army without due process of law, and wherein no conflict of jurisdiction between the military court and the civil court is involved. In fact, no military court is claiming jurisdiction over the persons of the petitioners. [They are simply being detained].[55]

In spite of the apparent soundness of those in dissent the opinion of the majority, as previously stated, was that United States military personnel were exempt from the jurisdiction of the courts of the Philippines.[56]

Although the *Raquiza* case was decided in September 1945, after the formal surrender of Japan, it should be noted that the Court held that the war had not terminated, maintaining that

> it is necessary to refer to a public act of the Executive Department to fix the date of the closing of the war... War, in the legal sense, continues until, and terminates at the time of, some formal proclamation of peace by an authority competent to proclaim it.[57]

The doctrine set forth by the Court in *Raquiza* v. *Bradford*, therefore, applied only to the period prior to the formal closing of the war. The Court in fact explicitly stated: "Whether the doctrine here laid down would be applicable to cases arising in time of peace, we do not decide."[58] In view of this explicit statement a later case, the *Tubb* case,

[54] See *ibid.*, pp. 63–76, concurred in by Justice Parás.

[55] *Ibid.*, pp. 72–74. Justice Perfecto's dissent noted: "There is no analogy between that of a foreign army which is granted free passage in a friendly country and that of the American Army in the Philippines, which has belonged here since the American flag began to fly in this country." The United States Army, Perfecto insisted, is not a "foreign army" but rather a "domestic army." *Ibid.*, p. 93.

[56] Only the relevant parts of the minority opinions have been mentioned. They argued equally well that the war was over in the Philippines, that the Commonwealth government had been restored and that the Constitution was in full force, hence the petitioners were being denied due process of law, and that even if the war were not over, the petitioners were being denied due process because they were being "detained" without trial and with no trial contemplated.

[57] *Raquiza* v. *Bradford*, 75 Phil. 50, 58 (1945), quoting *United States* v. *Tubig*, 3 Phil. 244, 254 (1904).

[58] *Raquiza* v. *Bradford*, 75 Phil. 50, 63 (1945).

becomes of importance. The alleged offense in this case occurred after Philippine independence was granted in July 1946, and apparently after the war was formally ended on December 31, 1946, but before the Military Bases Agreement of 1947 came into effect.[59]

George L. Tubb and Wesley Tedrow, citizens of the United States and residents of the Philippines, had signed contracts with the United States Army in Manila which stated, among other things, that they "voluntarily submitted themselves to United States military law while serving said contract..." In January 1947 they were apprehended by military authorities and charged before a general court-martial with

> violation of Articles of War regarding misappropriation of United States Government property destined for military use, said acts having been committed within premises occupied by the United States Army under lease contracts.[60]

In an original action before the Supreme Court of the Philippines the two men petitioned for a writ of habeas corpus, alleging that they were being "unlawfully deprived of their liberty" and that the Philippine courts had "exclusive jurisdiction over their arrest, confinement and imprisonment," because (1) they were not subject to military law and (2) martial law was no longer in force in the Philippines. The Court[61] noted the voluntary nature of the contracts, whereby Tubb and Tedrow had submitted "themselves to the full extent of the authority of the United States Army in this area." It held that the contracts, plus the fact that the petitioners were American citizens, made "their position during the subsistence of said contract no different from that of enlisted men, enlistment after all being nothing more than a contract of voluntary service in the armed forces of one's country." Thus, it was stated, the petitioners "can be deemed to possess the status of military personnel." The Court continued by stating that a foreign army allowed to be stationed in a friendly country is exempt from the civil and criminal jurisdiction of that country.[62] The basis of the Court's decision that such military personnel were exempt from Philippine jurisdiction was the opinion of Chief Justice Marshall in the United States case of *Schooner Exchange* v. *McFadden*.[63] Here Marshall stated:

[59] *Tubb and Tedrow* v. *Griess*, 78 Phil. 249 (1947). Tubb and Tedrow were charged before a general court-martial on January 28, 1947. The Court, however, did not state whether a state of war still existed at the time of the alleged offense. The silence of the Court apparently meant that the time of the commission of the offense, insofar as whether it occurred before or after December 31, 1946, was not of importance.

[60] *Ibid.*, p. 250.

[61] The majority opinion was written by Justice Moran, with eight other justices concurring. One other justice concurred in the result only, and one justice dissented.

[62] *Ibid.*

[63] *Schooner Exchange* v. *McFadden and Others*, 7 Cranch (U.S.) 116 (1812).

The grant of a free passage... implies a waiver of all jurisdiction over the troops during their passage, and permits the foreign general to use that discipline, and to inflict those punishments which the government of his army may require.[64]

The Philippine Court held that since the time of the *Schooner Exchange*, "this principle has been consistently embodied in treaties of military character among friendly nations and has been accepted by all the countries of the world."[65] The Court, however, cited no treaties.[66] In fact, there are few such treaties and certainly the "principle" had not been, nor is it now, accepted by all the countries of the world.[67] Contrary to the interpretation of the Court, the overwhelming majority of modern commentators maintain that no such general immunity of the visiting forces from the criminal jurisdiction of the foreign state exists in international law.[68]

[64] As quoted in *Tubb and Tedrow* v. *Griess*, 78 Phil. 249, 252 (1947).

[65] *Ibid.*

[66] A great majority of the agreements in which the visiting states have obtained exclusive jurisdiction over their forces have been concluded for wartime purposes, and most of these have involved agreements in which either the United States or Great Britain was the party receiving such jurisdiction over its forces. See, for example, United States-Belgium agreement of September 6, 1918, U.S., Department of State, *The World War*, in *Papers Relating to the Foreign Relations of the United States: 1918* (Washington: Government Printing Office, 1933), Supp. 2, pp. 747–748, 751; United States-France agreement of January 14, 1918, *ibid.*, pp. 735–737; Great Britain-France agreement of December 15, 1915, *ibid.*, p. 737; United States-Great Britain agreement of July 27, 1942, U.S., Department of State, *Executive Agreement Series* (1942), No. 355; United States-India agreement of September 29 and October 10, 1942, *ibid.*, No. 392; United States-Egypt agreement of March 2, 1943, *Executive Agreement Series* (1943), No. 356; United States-China agreement of May 21, 1943, *ibid.*, No. 360; United States-Belgium agreement (with respect to the Belgium Congo) of August 4, 1943, *ibid.*, No. 395; Great Britain- China agreement of July 7, 1945, 14 *United Nations Treaty Series* 445 (1948). In the pre-World War II period Great Britain was able to obtain exclusive jurisdiction over her forces in Iraq and Egypt, but these are special cases. See Great Britain-Iraq agreement of October 10, 1922, *Great Britain Treaty Series* (1925), No. 17; and Great Britain-Egypt agreement of August 26, 1936, *Great Britain Treaty Series* (1937), No. 6. Besides the United States and Great Britain, however, few countries have been able to obtain exclusive jurisdiction over their armed forces in friendly countries, even in times of war. For a discussion of these agreements and others, most of which do not provide for exclusive jurisdiction, see in particular Sung Yoon Cho, "Criminal Jurisdiction over Visiting Friendly Armed Forces, with Special Reference to Anglo-American Practice" [hereafter "Visiting Friendly Armed Forces"] (unpublished Master's thesis, Dept. of Political Science, Tulane University, 1957); and the three articles by G. P. Barton cited below, note 68.

[67] An additional criticism of the Court's opinion is that Chief Justice Marshall in the *Exchange* case referred only to the "passage" and not the "stationing" of troops in a friendly foreign country. This also is true of three of the numerous "authoritative writers on International Law" whom the Court cited. Lawrence, *Principles of International Law*, 6th ed., section 107, p. 246; McNair and Lauterpacht, *Annual Digest*, 1927–1928, Case No. 114; Vattel, III, section 130, as quoted in Woolsey's *International Law*, 6th ed., section 68. The strength of the support of a fourth authority is not clear, because no reference is made to "passage" or to "stationing" but only to "entering." Hyde, I *International Law*, section 247. Another states that "it is believed" that the visiting friendly force has exclusive criminal jurisdiction over its personnel. Hall, *International Law*, 7th ed., section 56. Only one of the writers cited appears to offer substantial support for the opinion of the majority. Wheaton, *Elements of International Law*, section 95.

[68] In concluding his study of the subject, G. P. Barton stated: "The examination of the

Justice Perfecto, in his dissent in the *Tubb* case, not only pointed out numerous alleged misinterpretations of the sources relied upon by the majority but also maintained that the "fundamental rights" of Tubb and Tedrow could not be "proper subjects of contracts." He enumerated the guaranteed rights in the Philippine Constitution and stated:

All these constitutional guarantees are intended to protect not only Filipino citizens, but all human beings within the territory of our Republic, including American citizens and, if need be, even against their own government and army.

At one point in his one-man dissent, Justice Perfecto pointed out:

This is one more case in which, by majority vote, this Supreme Court abdicated its powers, denying the victims of the redress to which they are entitled. In this case the abdication of judicial power is aggravated by a surrender of the sovereignty of the Filipino people. Without the benefit of ambassadorial negotiations, of senatorial ratifications, or even of a scrap of treaty or convention, the majority, in fact, accept and recognize extra-territoriality... No dissent is vigorous enough against such judicial attitude.[69]

In spite of the appeal of Perfecto, however, the Philippine Supreme Court denied the habeas corpus petition of Tubb and Tedrow, and in so doing recognized the right of the United States to exercise exclusive jurisdiction over its military personnel after the Philippines obtained independence and after the war formally ended.

Notwithstanding its decisions pertaining to jurisdiction over United

available evidence would appear to support the conclusion that there is no basis for a supposed rule of international law recognizing immunity from prosecution in local courts for members of a visiting force who commit offences either within the limits of their quarters, or while on duty, or against fellow servicemen or their property." Barton, "Foreign Armed Forces: Qualified Jurisdictional Immunity," 31 *British Yearbook of International Law* [hereafter *BYIL*] 341, 370 (1954). This study by Barton appears to offer the best treatment of the subject. See also Barton, "Foreign Armed Forces: Immunity from Supervisory Jurisdiction," 26 *BYIL* 380 (1949); Barton, "Foreign Armed Forces: Immunity from Criminal Jurisdiction," 27 *BYIL* 186 (1950); Bert A. Abrams, "International Law and Friendly Foreign Forces," Note, 32 *New York University Law Review* 351 (1957); Cho, "Visiting Friendly Armed Forces"; Note, "Criminal Jurisdiction over American Armed Forces Abroad," 70 *Harvard Law Review* 1043 (1957); Lester B. Orfield, "Jurisdiction of Foreign Courts over Crimes Committed Abroad by American Military Personnel," 8 *South Carolina Law Quarterly* 346 (1956); Edward D. Re, "The NATO Status of Forces Agreement and International Law," 50 *Northwestern University Law Review* 349 (1955); Vicente G. Reyes, "A Note on Jurisdiction over Friendly Foreign Armed Forces," 3 *Philippine International Law Journal* [hereafter *PILJ*] 133 (1964); Angel S. Salcedo, Manuel V. Reyes, and Claro C. Gloria, *The Armed Forces and the Law* (Quezon City: Capitol Publishing House, Inc., 1958), pp. 570–573. The opinion stated in a memorandum of the United States Attorney General is similar to that of Barton. See "International Law and the Status of Forces Agreement," 99 *Congressional Record* (Part 7) 8762 (July 14, 1953). The Supreme Court of the United States currently follows the view that there is no such general immunity. See *Wilson* v. *Girard*, 354 U.S. 524 (1957). For the contrary view to the opinions of those cited above, see Archibald King, "Jurisdiction over Friendly Foreign Armed Forces," 36 *American Journal of International Law* [hereafter *AJIL*] 539 (1942); and King, "Further Developments Concerning Jurisdiction over Friendly Forces," 40 *AJIL* 266 (1946).

[69] *Tubb and Tedrow* v. *Griess,* 78 Phil. 249, 258–259 (1947).

States military personnel, the Philippine Supreme Court, by a unanimous decision, ruled quite differently with respect to a case involving a Filipino. In *Valdez* v. *Lucero,* the case in point, murder allegedly had been committed in January 1945 by Valdez, a Filipino member of the guerrilla forces. Valdez was charged with murder in a civil court, but he maintained that the civil court was without jurisdiction. On appeal to the Supreme Court he claimed that the alleged crime had been committed at a place overrun by the Japanese forces and that, therefore, he should be tried by court-martial. In its opinion the Court stated:

> Granting all the facts alleged by the petitioner and that he was a regular member of the guerrilla [forces] duly recognized by the United States Army and granting further that his unit was incorporated into the United States Army, thus giving him the standing of a regular member of the United States armed forces, and that he was subsequently incorporated into the Philippine Army, we are of the opinion, nevertheless, that the civil courts of the Commonwealth of the Philippines are not deprived of their jurisdiction over the petitioner herein, but have concurrent jurisdiction with the military courts or general courts-martial to try and take cognizance of the case of murder...[70]

A comparison of the *Raquiza* and *Tubb* cases with the *Valdez* case demonstrates that it was not military personnel per se but only American military personnel that were outside the jurisdiction of the Philippine courts.

Summary

As has been seen in the above discussion, the jurisdictional arrangements that prevailed in the Philippines from 1898 to 1947 led to numerous conflicts of jurisdiction between the civil and military authorities. It also has been pointed out in the Brownell and *Hirshberg* cases that difficulties arose concerning offenses over which neither the civil nor the military authorities had jurisdiction.

Except for the brief period of the Spanish-American War, the three years of the Japanese occupation, and the period after the granting of Philippine independence, the jurisdictional arrangements were govern-

[70] *Valdez* v. *Lucero,* 76 Phil. 356, 360 (1946). It appears to be of significance that the Court did not find it necessary to inquire as to whether Valdez was simply a guerrilla, a member of a recognized guerrilla force, a member of the United States Army, or a member of the Philippine Army. Apparently the category was immaterial to the case. It should also be pointed out that the *Valdez* case appears to have modified, at least with respect to murder cases, the Philippine doctrine set forth in *United States* v. *Colley* [3 Phil. 58 (1903)] that "in time of war, insurrection or rebellion an officer or soldier cannot be tried at all in a civil court for an offense committed in the territory or district where the war, insurrection or rebellion exists." See Emiliano R. Navarro, *A Treatise on the Law of Criminal Procedure in the Philippines* (Manila: Diliman Publishing Co., 1952), p. 72.

ed by United States municipal law. For purposes of analysis the peace time arrangements may be viewed as revealing two basic jurisdictional patterns, one civil-oriented and the other military-oriented. If a civil-oriented arrangement is defined as one in which the general rule is concurrent jurisdiction over military personnel for offenses which are violations of both the civil and the military law, evidence of a civil-oriented pattern in the Philippines can be found in the United State Supreme Court decision in *Grafton* v. *United States*, the Philippine Supreme Court decision in the *Payomo* case, and the criminal jurisdictional arrangements, in general, during most of the colonial period. If departure from the general rule of concurrent jurisdiction over military personnel in the form of increased military jurisdiction is considered to be a military-oriented jurisdictional arrangement, evidence of a military-oriented pattern in the Philippines can be found in Executive Order Number 50 of 1912, Executive Order Number 151 of 1938, and the postwar Philippine Supreme Court decisions in the *Raquiza* and *Tubb* cases. A further example of a military-oriented pattern can be seen in the attempt of the naval authorities at Subic Bay to assert jurisdiction over civilians in 1920.[71] Of the two, the military-oriented pattern appeared to be paramount in the Philippines immediately before and immediately after World War II.[72]

[71] See, for example, the 1922 statement in U.S. Department of the Navy, *Laws Relating to the Navy*, pp. 63–64, where it is pointed out that in peace time "Congress have no power, and never had, to subject a person not in the military or naval service of the United States to a trial by court-martial for any crime..."

[72] Although involving a different status, the jurisdictional arrangements during the war and insurrection of 1898–1902 and the Japanese occupation may also be considered as factors involved in the military-oriented pattern.

CHAPTER II

ARRANGEMENTS FOR POSTWAR BASES IN THE PHILIPPINES

Prior to World War II the United States and the Philippines had agreed to eliminate almost completely United States bases in the Philippines after the granting of independence. When the Philippines became independent in 1946, however, the two countries mutually agreed that due to the effects of the war, it was necessary, to retain United States bases in the Philippines. This chapter will discuss both the pre-independence developments regarding the retention of the bases and the post-independence negotiations which led to the signing of the Military Bases Agreement of 1947.

Pre-Independence Developments—Background to Negotiations

Hare-Hawes-Cutting Act of 1933. As was noted in Chapter I, the President of the United States under the authority granted him by the Organic Act of 1902 and the Jones Act of 1916, set aside land in the Philippines for numerous military and naval reservations.[1] However, no attempts were made to provide for the statutory post-independence status of these reservations until the drafting of the first independence act in 1933. This act, the Hare-Hawes-Cutting Act,[2] provided in section 3 for the turnover of "all the property and rights" of the United States to the proposed Commonwealth of the Philippine Islands "except such land or other property as has heretofore been designated by the President of the United States for military and other reservations of the Government of the United States..."[3] Section 2 further stated that

[1] 32 *Stat.* 691 (1902); 39 *Stat.* 545 (1916).

[2] 47 *Stat.* 761 (1933). This act was vetoed by President Hoover who felt that it was unfair to the Filipinos because: (1) the period for economic adjustment was too short; (2) there was no military force in the Philippines to maintain internal order besides that of the United States; and (3) the independence of the Philippines possibly would be threatened by external dangers. For Hoover's veto message, see U.S., Congress, House Document 254, 72nd Cong., 2d Sess. (1933). Congress, however, repassed the act over the President's veto. See Hayden, p. 357.

[3] 47 *Stat.* 761, 764 (1933).

the constitution formulated by the Filipinos to establish the Commonwealth had to

> contain provisions to the effect that, pending the final and complete withdrawal of the sovereignty of the United States over the Philippine Islands... the Philippine Islands recognizes the right of the United States to expropriate property for public uses, [and] to maintain military and other reservations and armed forces in the Philippines...[4]

According to these provisions the power of the United States to retain existing bases and to designate additional bases was to be extended into the Commonwealth period.

Section 10 of the Hare-Hawes-Cutting Act, however, stated that ten years after the Commonwealth came into existence

> the President of the United States shall by proclamation withdraw and surrender all rights of possession, supervision, jurisdiction, control, or sovereignty then existing and exercised by the United States in and over the territory and people of the Philippine Islands, including all military and other reservations of the Government of the United States in the Philippines (except such land or property reserved under section 5 as may be redesignated by the President of the United States not later than two years after the date of such proclamation), and, on behalf of the United States, shall recognize the independence of the Philippine Islands...[5]

This would mean that, at least theoretically, the President could extend United States base privileges into the indefinite future. This provision in particular was objected to strongly by a number of influential Filipinos, including President Quezon.[6] It was reported that "one of the basic reasons for ... Quezon's opposition to the Hare-Hawes-Cutting Act was the provision relating to American military bases in the Philippines after independence."[7] As a result of this opposition, the Philippine Legislature refused to accept the act under the provisions of section 17.[8]

Tydings-McDuffie Act of 1934. This refusal led to the passage by the United States Congress of the second independence act, the Tydings-McDuffie Act of 1934.[9] The new act contained only one change of substance from the provisions of the Hare-Hawes-Cutting Act. This change occurred in the controversial section 10. As in the Hare-Hawes-Cutting Act, section 10(a) of the Tydings-McDuffie Act provided that ten years after the inauguration of the new government the United

[4] *Ibid.*, pp. 761–762.
[5] *Ibid.*, p. 768.
[6] For Filipino criticisms of the Hare-Hawes-Cutting Act, see 78 *Congressional Record* 4831–4842 (1934).
[7] Sergio Osmeña [Vice-President of the Commonwealth government], *Philippines Free Press* [hereafter *Free Press*], August 20, 1960, p. 57.
[8] Section 17, Hare-Hawes-Cutting Act, 47 *Stat.* 761, 770.
[9] 48 *Stat.* 456 (1934).

States would grant independence to the Philippines. The second act, however, went on to state that the United States was to turn over "all military and other reservations of the Government of the United States in the Philippines (except such naval reservations and fueling stations as are reserved under section 5)..." It further provided in section 10(b) that

the President of the United States is hereby authorized and empowered to enter into negotiations with the government of the Philippine Islands, not later than two years after his proclamation recognizing the independence of the Philippine Islands, for the adjustment and settlement of all questions relating to naval reservations and fueling stations of the United States in the Philippine Islands, and pending such adjustment and settlement the matter of naval reservations and fueling stations shall remain in its present status.[10]

Thus the United States was to remove her army and relinquish the army reservations, the latter comprising a total of some 300,000 acres of land.[11] Naval bases and fueling stations were to be retained, but the United States agreed to enter into negotiations within two years after independence "to determine the feasibility of further maintenance of... [the United States] Navy in the islands."[12] Technically, the statute would have allowed the United States to retain her naval bases and fueling stations if no agreement were reached with the Philippines on the final disposition of them. The evidence seems to indicate, however, that the United States was planning to withdrawn from the Philippines within a short time after independence.[13] Certainly, section 11 of the act pointed in that direction by stating that the President, "at the earliest practicable date," was "to enter into negotiations with foreign powers with a view to the conclusion of a treaty for the perpetual neutralization of the Philippine Islands..."[14] The provisions set forth in the Tydings-McDuffie Act were accepted by the Philippines and apparently constituted the basis of United States-Philippine policy until the Japanese attack occurred in 1941.

The Effects of World War II. During the period following the Japanese invasion in early December the situation in the Philippines changed

[10] *Ibid.*, p. 463.

[11] See 78 *Congressional Record* 4831, 4835 (1934).

[12] *Ibid.*, p. 4834.

[13] President Quezon, for example, stated that "President Roosevelt readily agreed that the maintenance of military reservations in the Philippines after the proclamation of the Philippine Republic would, in itself, make the granting of independence a farce." Quezon, *The Good Fight* (New York: D. Appleton-Century, 1946), p. 157, as quoted in Milton Walker Meyer, "A Diplomatic History of the Philippine Republic" (unpublished Ph.D. dissertation, Dept. of History, Stanford University, 1959), p. 25, note 77.

[14] 48 *Stat.* 456, 463 (1934). See also George E. Taylor, *The Philippines and the United States* (New York: Frederick A. Praeger, 1964), pp. 67–68.

rapidly. On December 28, 1941, General MacArthur requested United States action to offset the "'crescendo of enemy propaganda' which was being used with 'deadly effectiveness' in the Philippines." In a "hastily prepared" proclamation President Roosevelt gave a "solemn pledge" to the people of the Philippines that their freedom would be redeemed and their independence "established and protected."[15]

Although Philippine officials realized that acceptance of United States protection would involve the existence of United States bases in their country, they saw no alternative. President Quezon's reaction to Roosevelt's message was later reported by Vice-President Osmeña, who was with Quezon on Corregidor under bombing when the message arrived. Osmeña asked Quezon what he thought of the message. The exchange of words which followed was:

> "The message is great and I subscribe to it." "But Mr. President," I said, "this American protection involves the existence of American bases in the Philippines. Do you favor them now?" "With the lesson of this war," he answered, "we cannot escape the necessity of accepting it."

Thus, according to Osmeña, "right there, in his quarters, it was agreed among us that we would support the establishment of military bases in the Philippines [after independence]."[16] The Philippine plea thereafter was "for independence coupled now with American security."[17] This security, which had been promised by President Roosevelt, was to become congressional policy in 1944.

When the United States learned that the Japanese government was going to grant independence to the Philippines in October 1943, the President requested what came to be Joint Resolution 93.[18] In an attempt to counteract the effects of the Japanese action, Joint Resolution 93, in section 1, reaffirmed the United States policy of independence for the Philippines and granted President Roosevelt the authority to advance the date of independence. More important for the present study, however, were the provisions of section 2. This section provided:

[15] Robert E. Sherwood, *Roosevelt and Hopkins* (rev. ed.; New York: The University Library, 1950), p. 454. See also 6 *Department of State Bulletin* 5 (1942).

[16] Osmeña, *Free Press*, August 20, 1960, p. 57. Prior to this statement by Osmeña little was known as to why President Quezon took an about face in allowing United States military bases in the Philippines after independence. It was generally suspected, however, that after the Japanese defeat of the Philippines, Quezon realized that only with United States assistance would the Philippines be able to defend herself. See Vicente Albano Pacis, "Politics of Our Time," in *Progress Magazine 1956*, (Manila: Manila Times Publishing Co., 1956), p. 30.

[17] Osmeña, *Free Press*, August 20, 1960, p. 57.

[18] R. D. Tanjuakio, "The U.S.-P.I. Military Bases Agreement," 30 *Philippine Law Journal* 599, 605 (1955).

After negotiations with the President of the Commonwealth of the Philippines or the President of the Filipino Republic, the President of the United States is hereby authorized by such means as he finds appropriate to withhold or to acquire and to retain such bases, necessary appurtenances to such bases, and the right incident thereto, in addition to any provided for by the [Tydings-McDuffie] Act of March 24, 1934, as he may deem necessary for the mutual protection of the Philippine Islands and of the United States.[19]

Thus the provision of the Tydings-McDuffie Act that called for the elimination of the United States army bases in the Philippines and possibly, in a short time, the naval bases, was eliminated under the impact of World War II.

That the Philippines was satisfied with this policy was shown by Osmeña's statement that Joint Resolution 93 was approved by the United States Congress "in full consultation with the representatives of the Commonwealth government in Washington and after securing their full concurrence."[20] On May 14, 1945, President Osmeña[21] signed an agreement with President Truman that permitted the United States "to have military and naval bases in the islands."[22] Of the agreement Truman later said:

The Philippine Islands are a vital strategic center in the Pacific, and we were anxious that a military agreement with the Philippines be concluded in order that we might in the future continue to protect them against outside attack. The Filipinos themselves were equally anxious to have this protection, because without it the republic we were helping to establish might sometime find itself helpless.[23]

The agreement stated that

pending development of the detail plan, the U.S. will retain all sites which were held by the U.S. Army as military reservations on 7 December 1941 and by the U.S. Navy except at Cavite and will be accorded rights to sites in the localities shown on the attached Appendix.

The United States also was given the right to acquire "now" or "in the future" new sites if they were required.[24]

Upon his return to the Philippines after the liberation had begun, President Osmea "st ated that the military bases would be granted to

[19] 58 *Stat.* 625, 626 (1944).

[20] *Free Press*, August 20, 1960, p. 57. See also Taylor, p. 235; and Pacis, p. 30.

[21] Osmeña succeeded to the presidency upon the death of President Quezon on August 1, 1944.

[22] Harry S. Truman, *Years of Decision*, Vol. 1: *Memoirs* (Garden City, N.Y.: Doubleday and Co., Inc., 1955), p. 277. For the agreement, see "Manila Joint Staff Committee Report," Exhibit No. 26 (August 15, 1952), and 41 *Op.A.G.* 143, 153 (1953).

[23] Truman, p. 277. See also Sergio Osmeña, "Philippine Independence and U.S. Amity," 2 *Department of Foreign Affairs Review* 20, 20–23 (1956).

[24] As quoted in 41 *Op.A.G.* 143, 153 (1953).

the United States with the 'full support of the Filipino people.'"[25] Shortly thereafter the Philippine Congress, in its first postwar session, passed Joint Resolution Number 4, which "resolved that the Congress of the Philippines adheres to the policy and intent of Joint Resolution 93 (of the U.S. Congress)..." This resolution authorized the President of the Philippines to negotiate with the President of the United States for the establishment of United States bases in the Philippines.[26]

Independence and the Beginning of Negotiations

On July 4, 1946, Philippine independence was proclaimed by President Truman. On the same day the Treaty of General Relations between the United States and the Philippines was signed.[27] Article I of the treaty stated:

> The United States of America agrees to withdraw and surrender, and does hereby withdraw and surrender, all rights of possession, supervision, jurisdiction, control or sovereignty existing and exercised by the United States of America in and over the territory and the people of the Philippine Islands, except the use of such bases, necessary appurtenances to such bases, and the rights incident thereto, as the United States of America, by agreement with the Republic of the Philippines, may deem necessary to retain for the mutual protection of the United States of America and the Republic of the Philippines.

Thus, while independence was granted, provision also was made for the continuation of United States bases in the Philippines.

The treaty was proclaimed on October 22, 1946.[28] At this time, official Philippine opinion concerning the maintenance of the bases by the United States apparently was reflected well in a statement by President Roxas, Osmeña's successor to the presidency, when he stated: "It is my considered judgment... that by retaining our military ties with the United States we are serving first of all the interests of the Philippines."[29]

Both the Philippine independence proclamation issued by President Truman and the Treaty of General Relations called for military arrangements between the Philippines and the United States after independence. Joint Resolution 93 of the United States Congress and Joint Resolution 4 of the Philippine Congress furnished the constitutional

[25] As quoted in Meyer, p. 27.

[26] Joint Resolution No. 4, passed July 28, 1945. See 41 *Off. Gaz.* 349, 349–350 (1945).

[27] Treaty of General Relations, and Protocol. Signed at Manila July 4, 1946; entered into force October 22, 1946. 61 *Stat.* 1174; *TIAS* 1568.

[28] See Tanjuakio, p. 606.

[29] Roxas, *Important Speeches, Messages and Other Pronoucements* (Manila, 1947), pp. 196–197, as quoted in Meyer, p. 72.

authority for the conclusion of such arrangements. The former gave the President of the United States the authority to establish bases in the Philippines; the latter authorized the President of the Philippines to negotiate for such bases.

It should not be assumed, however, that the negotiations that took place occurred in a political vacuum. The dependence of the Philippines on the United States was an extremely influential factor. The Philippines had been hurt badly during the war, particularly during its latter stages when the Japanese were being driven from the islands.[30] Although Philippine independence was granted shortly after the allied victory, the Philippine leaders, as Taylor pointed out, "were completely dependent on the United States for assistance in restoring their economy and making good the damage that had been done to their buildings, communications, cities, plants, industries, and mines."[31] In addition, substantial agrarian unrest existed, especially in central Luzon. This was aggravated by the fact that large numbers of people were armed with weapons used during the war.[32]

The Philippines was facing a chaotic period not only internally but also on the international scene. Without United States assistance, Taylor maintained, she was "utterly defenseless." Even if the Filipinos desired to do so, he stated, this was no time "to insist on neutrality as a national policy or to resist the re-establishment of American bases on Philippine soil."[33] As Meyer has summarized: "The fluid international situation and weak domestic position [of the Philippines] necessitated protection."[34] As a result of these factors the Philippine leaders were anxious to obtain defense commitments from the United States.[35] Evidence indicates that the United States also was anxious to maintain strategic naval and air bases in the Philippines as part of her own defense arrangements.[36] Because of these strong mutual interests, negotiations for United States military bases in the Philippines

[30] See Carlos P. Romulo, *Crusade in Asia* (New York: John Day Co., 1955), chap. 1, and pp. 62–65; U.S. Department of State, *The Philippines* (Washington: Government Printing Office, 1951); George A. Malcolm, *First Malayan Republic* (Boston: Christopher House, 1951); and Paul O. Franson, Jr., "Implementation of the Report of the United States Economic Survey [Bell] Mission to the Philippines" (unpublished Master's thesis, Dept. of Political Science, Tulane University, 1955), chap. 1.

[31] Taylor, p. 113.

[32] See Romulo, pp. 93–95.

[33] Taylor, p. 113.

[34] Meyer, p. 24.

[35] See Sidney Shalett, *New York Times*, September 20, 1946, p. 11; Richard J. H. Johnson, *New York Times*, October 26, 1946, p. 6; and Taylor, pp. 112–114.

[36] See Sherwood, p. 792; Truman, p. 277; and the statement of General MacArthur, as reported in the *New York Times*, October 26, 1946, p. 6.

began shortly after the independence proclamation of July 1946.[37]

Negotiation of the Bases Agreement of 1947

In charge of the negotiating committees were Elpidio Quirino, Vice-President and at the same time Secretary of Foreign Affairs of the Philippines, and Ambassador Paul V. McNutt of the United States.[38] The negotiations were organized around a draft of a proposed agreement prepared by the United States government. This document, according to a statement by President Roxas, was "a draft based on what military experts felt at the time represented essential requirements for the mutual protection of the Philippines and the United States." During the seven-month period of negotiations "every paragraph, every sentence, and every phrase [of the draft proposal] were gone over, scrutinized and discussed."[39]

Little public discussion of the negotiations occurred until an October report in the Philippine press that four major points had been set forth by the Filipino negotiating committee.[40] First, the Philippine negotiators were insisting that there be no United States bases in the heavily populated areas of the Philippines, and particularly in Manila. Wilkins, of the *New York Times*, reported that the Philippine negotiators objected to close contact between the United States military personnel and large numbers of Filipinos because of the "likelihood of friction," because of the fear of having military installations in populous areas in an atomic warfare age, and because the Filipinos wanted to use certain

[37] Statement of President Roxas, 43 *Off. Gaz.* 954, 958 (1947). A United States Department of State official reported in early June 1946 that the discussions on the agreement had already begun. Edward W. Mill, "The Philippines Prepares for Independence," 14 *Department of State Bulletin* 980 (1946). See also Mill, "The New Republic of the Philippines," 15 *Department of State Bulletin* 475 (1946). Apparently, however, serious discussions did not begin until after independence was granted.

Most of the major source materials covering the negotiations of the 1947 agreement are not available. Two research studies have been undertaken. The latest is a thesis by Mr. James H. MacFarland, Jr., prepared for the Naval War College, Newport, Rhode Island, in 1965. This thesis discusses the 1947 agreement and subsequent negotiations, but it is classified secret because some of the source material used was so classified. Mr. MacFarland, personal letter dated February 25, 1966. The State Department earlier had conducted a research paper on "The Negotiation of the United States-Philippine Military Bases Agreement of 1947," Research Project No. 319, dated February 1953. This research project and the State Department files on the negotiations are classified and are not available. Mr. Eugene T. Herbert, Office of Legal Adviser, Department of State, personal letter dated December 10, 1965. The following is therefore highly tentative. It is based on unofficial press reports made during the period of the negotiations, later newspaper reports, and public statements by President Manuel Roxas, which were made immediately after the agreement was signed.

[38] Statement of President Roxas, 43 *Off. Gaz.* 952, 953 (1947); Meyer, p. 73.

[39] 43 *Off. Gaz.* 954, 957–958 (1947).

[40] See H. Ford Wilkins, *New York Times*, October 16, 1946, p. 8.

select industrial and commercial sites which the United States military desired to have.[41] It was reported by President Roxas that the insistence of the Philippine delegation on no military bases in large centers of population conflicted "sharply" with the plans of the United States Army. The United States, stated Roxas, wanted to fulfill her obligation as cheaply as possible, and "the Army had gone far in the preparation of its plans and in actual construction projects, with Manila as the center of the network of defense establishments."[42] Nevertheless, the Filipino delegation stood fast and was eventually successful on this issue.[43]

A second major concern of the Philippine delegation was that only "front-line bases and not auxiliary installations be considered..."[44] It is difficult to say how successful the Filipinos were in maintaining this position, primarily because of the problem of determining precisely what was meant by a "front-line" base. If one assumes, however, that front-line base was intended to mean operational base, the final agreement apparently reflected a compromise on this issue. It was reported by Senator Sebastian that the original American draft listed seventy bases for retention by the United States.[45] If this figure actually reflected the wishes of the United States, the final results represented a considerable compromise. President Roxas later expressed the view that the Philippine delegation had reached a satisfactory solution to this issue.[46]

A third point of dispute concerned whether or not American contractors on the United States bases should be subject to Philippine tax laws.[47] Little publicity was given to this issue. The final

[41] *Ibid.* Another reporter, Richard J. H. Johnston, stated that the "unanimous and unshakable opposition of the Philippine delegation" toward the establishment or retention of United States bases in Manila was "due in large measure to the unsavory behavior on the part of American troops." Johnston also noted that the establishment of bases in Manila would deprive Filipinos of "needed docking, warehousing and other commercial facilities." *New York Times*, October 26, 1946, p. 6. President Roxas later stated that the Philippines had insisted on no bases in large centers of population because it might "have been a breeding ground for friction and misunderstanding." 43 *Off. Gaz.* 954, 959 (1947).

[42] *Ibid.*

[43] See statement of President Roxas, 43 *Off. Gaz.* 952, 952 (1947); and *New York Times*, March 15, 1947, p. 1.

[44] William S. White, *New York Times*, December 13, 1946, p. 12.

[45] Senator Proceso Sebastian to the Senate, 2 [Philippine] *Congressional Record* 2181 (1947), as cited in Meyer, pp. 74–75. In his State of the Nation address of January 27, 1947, President Roxas hinted that the United States desired more bases than they were to receive under the 1947 agreement. 43 *Off. Gaz.* 195, 218 (1947).

[46] 43 *Off. Gaz.* 954, 961 (1947).

[47] See White, *New York Times*, December 13, 1946, p. 12; and Wilkins, *New York Times*, October 16, 1946, p. 8.

agreement, however, favored the view of the United States.[48]

The fourth major issue was that of jurisdiction. Apparently, from the beginning of the negotiations the Philippine delegation accepted the idea of extraterritorial rights for United States military personnel while on the bases. They were anxious, however, to limit these rights to the base areas.[49] As a result, the question in dispute involved off-base offenses. President Roxas correctly identified the essence of the problem when he noted:

> It is a fundamental doctrine in the armed services that a commanding officer must have complete control of his troops, especially in the matter of discipline. The very existence of an armed force depends on that general requirement. Nevertheless, [in the negotiations] we faced a situation in which the American troops were to be established on Philippine soil. The jurisdiction of our courts and of our laws had to be maintained.[50]

After long and intensive study, Roxas stated, an "eminently satisfactory" formula has been worked out which meets "both requirements of the military and the essential dignity of our sovereign jurisdiction. "In no true respect," he declared, "is extraterritoriality indicated or authorized."[51] Whether or not this statement by Roxas was true depends upon one's definition of extraterritoriality. However, the United States, as will be seen in the next chapter, clearly emerged in a favorable position insofar as jurisdiction was concerned.

Apparently all four of the points set forth above were resolved satisfactorily as the draft of the completed agreement had the approval of the whole Philippine panel.[52] With repect to the general course of the negotiations President Roxas reported that "considering the tremendous import of the subject matter," the negotiations had "at all times been harmonious and agreeable."[53] Several times during the negotiations it was reported that there had been no suggestion of "pressure"

[48] See Article XII of the Military Bases Agreement of 1947, which stated: "No national of the United States, or corporation organized under the laws of the United States, resident in the United States, shall be liable to pay income tax in the Philippines in respect of any profits derived under a contract made in the United States with the Government of the United States in connection with the construction, maintenance, operation and defense of the bases, or any tax in the nature of a license in respect of any service or work for the United States in connection with the construction, maintenance, operation and defense of the bases."

[49] Both Wilkins and White stated that the Philippines wanted to limit the extraterritorial rights of the United States to the bases. Wilkins, *New York Times*, October 16, 1946, p. 8; White, *New York Times*, December 13, 1946, p. 12.

[50] 43 *Off. Gaz.* 954, 960 (1947).

[51] *Ibid.*, p. 962.

[52] Statement of President Roxas, *ibid.*, p. 959.

[53] 43 *Off. Gaz.* 952, 952 (1947).

on the Philippine negotiators by the United States officials.[54] At one point, however, the United States "startled the Filipinos by offering to withdraw all their forces."[55] Although evidence is not available to establish the exact meaning of this "offer," there is some indication that it grew out of the view of some United States military officials that it would be best to withdraw from the Philippines and use other islands of the Western Pacific so that there would be no question of United States authority or jurisdiction.[56] It was reported, however, that President Roxas and Vice-President Quirino immediately rejected the offer.[57]

In his State of the Nation address of January 27, 1947, President Roxas seemed to indicate that the Philippines did not view this incident as a threat by the United States.[58] Nevertheless, one newspaper article stated that the United States offer to withdraw and the immediate rejection of the offer by the Philippines were "credited with strengthening the American bargaining position..."[59] If Philippine officials believed pressure was being exerted, they did not refer to it publicly.

On March 14, the United States and the Philippines signed the Military Bases Agreement of 1947. The Philippines apparently handled the agreement as a treaty and, under the provisions of section 10, paragraph 7 of the Philippine Constitution, submitted it to the Senate for approval. The discussion in the Senate seemed to indicate little dissatisfaction with either the agreement as a whole or the jurisdictional provisions in particular. Apparently the only Senator to oppose the agreement because of the jurisdictional arrangements was Senator Cabili who maintained that Philippine jurisdictional rights were being usurped.[60] In spite of this objection the agreement was approved for ratification by an 18–0 vote with three Senators absent.[61] Since the United States handled the agreement as an executive agreement, it was not submitted to the Senate for approval. No discussion of the agreement took place in Congress. On March 26, 1947, the Military Bases Agreement officially entered into force.

[54] See White, *New York Times*, December 13, 1946, p. 12; and *New York Times*, February 2, 1947, p. 24.

[55] *Ibid.* See also the statement of President Roxas, 43 *Off. Gaz.* 195, 217–218 (1947).

[56] See *New York Times*, December 3, 1946, p. 18.

[57] *Ibid.*, February 2, 1947, p. 24.

[58] 43 *Off. Gaz.* 195, at 217–218.

[59] *New York Times*, February 2, 1947, p. 24.

[60] Senator Tomas Cabili to the Senate. 2 [Philippine] *Congressional Record* 225 (1947), as cited in Meyer, p. 79.

[61] *Ibid.*, p. 78.

Summary

United States policy with respect to the proposed independent Republic of the Philippines was first set forth in the Hare-Hawes-Cutting Act of 1933. This act was rejected by the Philippine Legislature, primarily because it provided for the retention of United States naval and military bases in the Philippines after independence. The Tydings-McDuffie Act, passed in 1934, was similar to the 1933 act except that it provided for the turning over to the Philipines of all United States military bases in the Philippines.

Because of the effects of World War II, however, United States and Philippine leaders agreed that it would be mutually beneficial for the naval and military bases to be retained. Therefore, when Philippine independence was granted, it became necessary for the two countries to reach agreement on the status of these bases. Mainly due to Philippine dependence upon the United States, the Philippines was in a difficult position to obtain a favorable arrangement. Thus the negotiations led to an agreement which was advantegous to the United States particularly with respect to its criminal jurisdictional provisions. In spite of this, the Philippines expressed little dissatisfaction with the agreement at that time.

CHAPTER III

CRIMINAL JURISDICTION UNDER THE MILITARY BASES AGREEMENT OF 1947

The preamble of the Military Bases Agreement of 1947[1] clearly states that the war in the Pacific had confirmed the mutual interest of the United States and the Philippines "in matters relating to the defense of their respective territories." Further, it had prompted the two nations to provide for their common defense,

> particularly through a grant to the United States of America by the Republic of the Philippines in the exercise of its title and sovereignty, of the use, free of rent, in furtherance of the mutual interest of both countries, of certain lands of the public domain...

These grants of land were to be used for United States military bases according to the terms set forth in the agreement "for the delimitation, establishment, maintenance and operation of [such] military bases."

The 1947 agreement deals comprehensively with the rights and duties to which the two parties agree. This chapter, however, will set forth only briefly the general provisions of the agreement as background for an extended discussion of the criminal jurisdictional arrangements.

Base Arrangements in General

Under the provisions of Article I the United States maintained the right to retain the use of sixteen bases located in the Philippines and, upon notice, the right to use seven other bases as required by military necessity.[2] Article I further provides that the Philippines

[1] Agreement Concerning Military Bases, and Exchange of Notes. Signed at Manila March 14, 1947; entered into force March 26, 1947. 61 *Stat.* 4019; *TIAS* 1775.

[2] These bases were listed in, respectively, Annex A and Annex B. Of the sixteen bases listed in Annex A, President Roxas stated that there were "only seven listings of actual operational military bases in the acceptable meaning of the word." Three of these seven in Pampanga Province were contiguous and actually constituted only one base for the Army and the Air Force. The other four "operational" bases were the naval bases at Subic Bay, Sangley Point, and Tawi Tawi, Guiuan. The other nine bases listed in Annex A consisted of three installations for aids to navigation, one minor coast guard station, one radio station, one naval anchorage, one military cemetery, and one leave and recreation center. See statement of President Roxas, 43 *Off. Gaz.* 954, 961 (1947).

agrees to enter into negotiations at the request of the United States

to permit the United States to expand such bases, to exchange such bases for other bases, to acquire additional bases, or relinquish rights to bases, as any of such exigencies may be required by military necessity.

In addition to the above bases, it was provided in Article XXI, paragraph 1, that the United States retained

the right to occupy temporary quarters and installations now existing outside the bases..., for such reasonable time, not exceeding two years, as may be necessary to develop adequate facilities within the bases for the United States armed forces. If circumstances require an extension of time, such a period will be fixed by mutual agreement of the two Governments; but such extension shall not apply to the existing temporary quarters and installations within the limits of the City of Manila and shall in no case exceed a period of three years.

The provisions of paragraph 1 notwithstanding, paragraph 2 specially provided that the Port of Manila reservation was to be available to the United States "until such time as other arrangements can be made for supply of the bases by mutual agreement."

In the event that it becomes necessary to acquire private property located in the bases, the Philippines, according to Article XXII, agrees to institute and prosecute condemnation or expropriation proceedings "in accordance with the laws of the Philippines." The United States agrees "to reimburse the Philippines for all the reasonable expenses, damages and costs thereby incurred, including the value of the property as determined by the Court."

Article III grants the United States

the rights, power and authority within the bases which are necessary for the establishment, use, operation and defense thereof or appropriate for the control thereof and all the rights, power and authority within the limits of territorial water and air space adjacent to, or in the vicinity of, the bases which are necessary to provide access to them or appropriate for their control.

This grant of "rights, power and authority," paragraph 2 states, shall include, *inter alia*, the right, power and authority:

(a) to construct (including dredging and filling), operate, maintain, utilize, occupy, garrison and control the bases;

(b) to improve and deepen the harbors, channels, entrances and anchorages, and to construct or maintain necessary roads and bridges affording access to the bases;

(c) to control (including the right to prohibit) in so far as may be required for the efficient operation and safety of the bases, and within the limits of military necessity, anchorages, moorings, landings, takeoffs, movements and operation of ships and waterborne crafts, aircraft and other vehicles on water, in the air or on land comprising or in the vicinity of the bases...

As readily can be seen the United States is given rather extensive and, in many respects, vague rights both within and in the immediate vicinity of the bases.[3] It is provided in paragraph 3 of Article III, however, that "in the practical application outside the bases of the rights, power and authority granted in this Article there shall be, as the occasion requires, consultation between the two Governments."

Article VI provides that, subject to previous agreements with the Philippines, the United States has the right to use land and coastal areas "for periodic maneuvers, for additional staging areas, bombing and gunnery ranges, and for such intermediate airfields as may be required for safe and efficient air operations." It is further provided, in Article VII, that the United States has the right to the use of public services and utilities in the Philippines under conditions "no less favorable than those that may be applicable from time to time to the military forces of the Philippines."

The United States, in Article VIII, is granted the right, in cooperation with the appropriate authorities of the Philippines,

> to take such steps as may be mutually agreed upon to be necessary to improve health and sanitation in areas contiguous to the bases, including the right, under such conditions as may be mutually agreed upon, to enter and inspect any privately owned property.

It is further stated that the United States agrees to pay "just compensation" for injuries to persons or damages to property that result "from action taken in connection with the Article."

Under the provisions of Article V the United States receives exemption from Philippine customs and other duties. Article V states:

> No import, excise, consumption or other tax, duty or impost shall be charged on material, equipment, supplies or goods, including food stores and clothing, for exclusive use in the construction, maintenance, operation or defense of the bases, consigned to, or destined for, the United States authorities and certified by them to be for such purposes.

Article XVII states that the United States has the right "to remove or dispose of any or all removable improvements, equipment or facilities located at or on any base and paid for with funds of the United States," and that such removal will not be subject to any export tax. It further stipulates that

> the United States is not obligated to turn over the bases to the Philippines at the expiration of this Agreement or the earlier relinquishment of any bases in the condition in which they were at the time of their occupation, nor is the Philippines obliged to make any compensation to the United States for the improvements made

[3] The use of the term "*inter alia*" in Article III, the "Description of Rights" article, indicates the vagueness of how extensive the Philippine grants of rights, power, and authority might be.

in the bases or for the buildings or structures left thereon, all of which shall become the property of the Philippines upon the termination of the Agreement or the earlier relinquishment by the United States of the bases where the structures have been built.

The United States obtains the right to bring its personnel into the Philippines under the provisions of Article XI. This article states:

> It is mutually agreed that the United States shall have the right to bring into the Philippines members of the United States military forces and the United States nationals employed by or under a contract with the United States together with their families, and technical personnel of other nationalities (not being persons excluded by the laws of the Philippines) in connection with the construction, maintenance, or operation of the bases.

It also states that if the status of any such person changes "so that he would no longer be entitled to such admission," the United States is to notify the Philippines, and if the Philippines requires such a person to leave the country, the United States is responsible for providing him "with a passage from the Philippines within a reasonable time," and is in the meantime to prevent his becoming a "public responsibility" of the Philippines.

Under the provisions of Article XII, United States military personnel and their dependents and other United States nationals and their dependents "serving in or employed in the Philippines in connection with the construction, maintenance, operation or defense of the bases" are exempted from the payment of income tax in the Philippines, except for income derived from Philippine sources. The same personnel are exempted from the payment of "any poll or residence tax, or any import or export duty, or any other tax on personal property imported for his own use..." It further states:

> No national of the United States, or corporation organized under the laws of the United States, resident in the United States, shall be liable to pay income tax in the Philippines in respect of any profits derived under a contract made in the United States with the Government of the United States in connection with the construction, maintenance, operation and defense of the bases, or any tax in the nature of a license in respect of any service or work for the United States in connection with the construction, maintenance, operation and defense of the bases.

To provide for the security of the bases, the Philippines, in Article XV, agrees

> to take such steps as may from time to time be agreed to be necessary with a view to the enactment of legislation to insure the adequate security and protection of the United States bases, equipment and other property and the operations of the United States under this Agreement, and the punishment of persons who may contravene such legislation.

Under the provisions of Article XXV the Philippines agrees that no base will be granted to a third power without the consent of the United

States, and the United States agrees that it will not, without the consent of the Philippines, "assign, or underlet, or part with the possession of the whole or any part of any base, or of any right, power, or authority by this Agreement, to any third power."

The agreement, according to Article XXIX, was to enter into force upon its acceptance by the two governments and remain in force for a period of ninety-nine years "subject to extension thereafter as agreed by the two Governments."

Criminal Jurisdictional Arrangements

The major aspects of the criminal jurisdictional arrangements were found in Article XIII. The following discussion will set forth the basic provisions of that article. Several other articles which were of ancillary importance to the jurisdictional arrangements also will be included.

The Right to Exercise Criminal Jurisdiction. Under the provisions of paragraph 1 of the 1947 agreement the Philippines consented that the United States had the right to exercise jurisdiction over the following offenses:

(a) Any offense committed by any person within any base except where the offender and offended parties are both Philippine citizens (not members of the armed forces of the United States on active duty) or the offense is against the security of the Philippines;

(b) Any offense committed outside the bases by any member of the armed forces of the United States in which the offended party is also a member of the armed forces of the United States; and

(c) Any offense committed outside the bases by any member of the armed forces of the United States against the security of the United States.

Paragraph 2 stated that the Philippines had the right to exercise jurisdiction "over all other offenses committed outside the bases by any member of the armed forces of the United States." Thus, the jurisdictional arrangements were established on the basis of a combination of territorial and nationality principles.

As can be seen, these provisions did not use the terms "exclusive jurisdiction," "concurrent jurisdiction," or "the primary right to exercise jurisdiction," terms that later were used in the NATO Status of Forces Agreement (SOFA).[4] From the text of paragraph 3 and paragraph 4 it appears that each of the parties to the Philippine agreement had exclusive jurisdiction in its respective jurisdictional area unless positive action was taken to the contrary. Paragraph 3 stated:

[4] See below, pp. 41–42.

Whenever for special reasons the United States may desire not to exercise the jurisdiction reserved to it... ,the officer holding the offender in custody shall so notify the fiscal (prosecuting attorney) of the city or province in which the offense has been committed within ten days after his arrest, and in such a case the Philippines shall exercise jurisdiction.

Paragraph 4 used similar language in providing for cases in which the Philippines desired to waive its rights to exercise jurisdiction, as "reserved" under the provisions of paragraph 2. Thus, the provisions of both paragraphs seemed to require that positive action to waive jurisdiction be taken by the party to whom jurisdiction was reserved before the other party could exercise jurisdiction.

In addition to the rights granted to the United States under paragraph 1, paragraph 4 provided that the United States had the right to exercise jurisdiction over members of its armed forces for off-base offenses committed "(a) while [the offender was] engaged in the actual performance of a specific military duty, or (b) during a national emergency declared by either Government..." The Philippine authorities, however, had the right to determine whether or not an off-base offense had occurred while the offender was engaged in the performance of a specific military duty or during a period of national emergency. This determination, according to paragraph 4(b), was to be made by the fiscal (prosecuting attorney) concerned with the particular case. If the fiscal found that the offense occurred while the offender was engaged in the actual performance of a specific duty or during a period of national emergency, he was required to notify immediately the United States officer holding the offender in custody that the United States was free to exercise jurisdiction. If the fiscal concluded that the offense had not occurred while the offender was in the performance of a specific duty or during a national emergency, the offender's commanding officer could appeal to the Philippine Secretary of Justice, whose decision was final.

It should be noted that the Philippine right to determine whether or not an offense occurred in the performance of duty differed from the provisions of the NATO SOFA. No specific statement is made in the NATO agreement as to whether the sending or the receiving state would make such a determination, but, as Snee and Pye noted, it is clear from the "working papers" that the negotiators of the NATO SOFA contemplated that the military authorities of the sending state would make the determination.[5]

[5] Snee and Pye, p. 51. Since the agreement was "silent" on this point, it has been neces-

Paragraph 6 of the United States-Philippine agreement contained a final provision pertaining to the right of the United States to exercise jurisdiction. According to this paragraph, the United States had the right to exercise exclusive jurisdiction over members of its armed forces in time of war, the other provisions of Article XIII notwithstanding.

Custody. In cases in which the Philippines desired to exercise jurisdiction, it was provided in paragraph 5 that the "custody of the accused, pending trial and final judgment, shall be entrusted without delay to the commanding officer of the nearest base..." It was further stated that in such cases the commanding officer receiving an accused "shall acknowledge in writing" that the accused would be produced before court when so requested. In addition, paragraph 5 provided that the commanding officer "shall be furnished by the fiscal... with a copy of the information [complaint] against the accused upon the filing of the original in the competent court."

Arrest and Service of Process. In addition to the provisions of Article XIII, paragraphs 1 and 2 of Article XIV also are of importance with respect to criminal jurisdiction. According to the terms of paragraph 1 no arrest can be made "and no process, civil or criminal, shall be served within any base except with the permission of the commanding officer of such base..." If, however, the commanding officer refuses to grant this permission

> he shall (except in cases of arrest where the United States has jurisdiction under Article XIII) forthwith take the necessary steps to arrest the person charged and surrender him to the appropriate authorities of the Philippines or to serve such process, as the case may be, and to provide the attendance of the server of such process before the appropriate court in the Philippines or procure such server to make the necessary affidavit or declaration to prove such service as the case may require.

In cases in which the United States had jurisdiction under Article XIII, paragraph 2 of Article XIV provided for the Philippines to give, on request, "reciprocal facilities as regards the service of process and the arrest and surrender of alleged offenders." It is important to note that paragraph 7 of Article XIII specifically stated that the United States "agrees that it will not grant asylum in any of the bases to any person fleeing from the lawful jurisdiction of the Philippines." It further provided that if any such person was found in any base, "he will be surrendered on demand to the competent authorities of the Philippines."

sary "to obtain the acquiescence of each receiving State individually for the exercise of this right by the sending State." *Ibid.* For the working arrangements in the NATO countries, see *ibid.*, pp. 51–54.

Civil Jurisdiction. Although this study is concerned primarily with the criminal jurisdictional arrangements in the Philippines, some mention should be made of the civil jurisdictional arrangements. Under the agreement of 1947 these arrangements are found in Article XIII, paragraph 8 and in Article XXIII. The latter states:

For the purpose of promoting and maintaining friendly relations by the prompt settlement of meritorious claims, the United States shall pay just and reasonable compensation, when accepted by claimants in full satisfaction and in final settlement, for claims, including claims of insured but excluding claims of subrogees, on account of damage to or loss or destruction of private property, both real and personal, or personal injury or death of inhabitants of the Philippines, when such damage, loss, destruction or injury is caused by the armed forces of the United States, or individual members thereof, including military or civilian employees thereof, or otherwise incident to non-combat activities of such forces; provided that no claim shall be considered unless presented within one year after the occurrence of the accident or incident out of which such claim arises.

Should this procedure or the compensation offered not be satisfactory to a claimant in cases in which the United States exercises criminal jurisdiction, the courts of the Philippines remain open. In such cases, paragraph 8 of Article XIII states that

the offended party may institute a separate civil action against the offender in the proper court of the Philippines to enforce the civil liability which under the laws of the Philippines may arise from the offense.

As has been noted previously, Article XIV, paragraph 1, provides that no civil process can be served within any base by Philippine authorities "except with the permission of the commanding officer of such base..." If the commanding officer refuses to grant such permission, he is obligated to take the necessary steps to see that the process is served.[6] Apparently, the Philippine authorities are free to serve such process if the proposed recipient is off base.[7]

Major Differences between the NATO SOFA and the Philippine Agreement

Several of the provisions for the right to exercise criminal jurisdiction under the Military Bases Agreement of 1947 were significantly different

[6] All of the above provisions pertaining to civil jurisdiction remain in effect under the 1965 agreement.

[7] Of related interest is the case of the *Sitka*. In this case Attorney General Cushing in 1855 ruled that the courts of California had no jurisdiction to issue a writ of *habeas corpus* to the commanding officer of a British prize, the *Sitka*, to bring up a prisoner of war held on board. Cushing stated that the commanding officer of the vessel "might have made a return to the writ of *habeas corpus*, 'if he had service of it whilst on shore.'" 7 *Op.A.G.* 122, 130 (1855), as quoted in David R. Deener, *The United States Attorneys General and International Law* (The Hague: Martinus Nijhoff, 1957), p. 242. For further comment on the case, see *ibid.*, pp. 242, 345–346.

from those which later were established under the NATO SOFA.[8] These differences became of major importance to the Filipinos and contributed substantially to their dislike of the 1947 agreement.

The most basic difference between the provisions of the Philippine agreement and the NATO SOFA was that the former, with a few exceptions, designated the right to exercise jurisdiction on the basis of where the offense occurred, inside the base or outside the base, while the latter designated this right on the basis of the status of the offender and the status of the offended with no distinction being made between offenses committed on base or off base. The NATO SOFA provides in paragraph 2(a) that the sending state

> shall have the right to exercise exclusive jurisdiction over persons subject to the military law of that State with respect to offenses... punishable by the law of the sending State, but not by the law of the receiving State.

Similar provisions are set forth in paragraph 2(b) with respect to the right to exercise exclusive jurisdiction by the receiving state. In all other cases the right to exercise jurisdiction is concurrent. In an attempt to eliminate conflicts of jurisdiction, paragraphs 3(a) and 3(b) establish criteria for determining which state has the primary right to exercise jurisdiction in situations involving concurrent jurisdiction. These criteria are as follows:

> (a) The military authorities of the sending State shall have the primary right to exercise jurisdiction over a member of a force or of a civilian component in relation to
> (i) offenses solely against the property or security of that State, or offenses solely against the person or property of another member of the force or civilian component of that State or of a dependent;
> (ii) offenses arising out of any act or omission done in the performance of official duty.
> (b) In the case of any other offense the authorities of the receiving State shall have the primary right to exercise jurisdiction.

Thus, as indicated previously, the NATO SOFA makes no distinction between criminal offenses committed on base and those committed off base. In addition, paragraph 4 of the NATO SOFA explicitly states that the sending state is prohibited from exercising jurisdiction "over persons who are nationals of or ordinarily resident in the receiving State, unless they are members of the force of the sending State."

In contrast, by designating the right to exercise jurisdiction almost solely on the basis of the place in which the offense occurred, the Philip-

[8] NATO SOFA. Signed at London June 19, 1951; entered into force for the United States August 23, 1953. 4 *UST* 1792; *TIAS* 2846. The criminal jurisdictional arrangements are found in Article VII. All of the provisions pertaining to the NATO SOFA in this chapter are still in effect.

pine agreement allowed the United States to exercise jurisdiction over Filipinos for offenses committed on the bases, unless the offense was committed against another Filipino or against Philippine national security. Apparently, the United States-Philippine agreement of 1947 was the only peace time status of forces agreement in which the sending state had the right to exercise jurisdiction over nationals of the receiving state.[9] From the viewpoint of the Filipinos the right of the United States to exercise such jursidiction became one of the most objectionable aspects of the 1947 agreement.

Another complaint which arose out of the determining of jurisdiction on the basis of whether the offense was committed on or off base was that the Philippines could not exercise jurisdiction over crimes committed on the bases by United States personnel, no matter against whom the crime was committed, unless the United States military authorities decided to waive their right to exercise jurisdiction.[10] The NATO SOFA, in paragraphs 3(a) and 3(b), provides that the authorities of the receiving state have primary jurisdiction over personnel of the sending state for offenses committed against a national of the receiving state (or against a third party), unless the offense arose out of an act or omission done in the performance of official duty. Thus, for example, an on-base offense by a member of the United States forces against a national of the receiving state is subject to the jurisdiction of the receiving state under the NATO agreement but not under the Philippine agreement. This distinction between the NATO provisions and the provisions of the United States-Philippine agreement, although of little importance in the early years of the agreement, later came to be the major Filipino objection.

In still another area the provisions of the Philippine agreement differed from those of the NATO SOFA. This area concerned investi-

[9] Even the agreements that are published between the Soviet Union and several of the Eastern European countries do not provide for trial of nationals of the receiving state by the military authorities of the Soviet Union. For the published agreements, see 52 *AJIL* 210, 210–227 (1958): Agreement Concerning Questions Connected with the Presence of Soviet Forces on East German Territory, signed at Berlin March 12, 1957, in force April 27, 1957; Agreement on the Legal Status of the Soviet Forces Temporarily Present on the Territory of the Hungarian People's Republic, signed at Budapest May 27, 1957 [no statement as to when in force]; Agreement on the Legal Status of Soviet Forces Temporarily Stationed in Poland, signed at Warsaw December 17, 1956, in force February 27, 1957. The criminal jurisdictional arrangements of each of these agreements follow closely those of the NATO SOFA, except that in Hungary and Poland the trial of members of the Soviet forces by the receiving state are to be by the military administrators of justice of the receiving state.

[10] There is one possible exception to this statement. A literal interpretation of paragraph 1(a) would allow the Philippines to exercise jurisdiction over any offense—whether committed by an American or a Filipino—against Philippine national security, whether committed on or off the bases. No such case, however, has arisen.

gations into alleged offenses and the collection and handing over of evidence relative to such offenses. Article VII, paragraph 6(a) of the NATO SOFA provides:

> The authorities of the receiving and sending States shall assist each other in the carrying out of all necessary investigations into offenses, and in the collection and production of evidence, including the seizure and, in proper cases, the handing over of objects connected with an offense.

The United States-Philippine agreement had no such provision. Article XX of the agreement, however, does call for

> close cooperation on a reciprocal basis between the military and naval police forces of the United States and the police forces of the Philippines for the purpose of preserving order and discipline among United States military and naval personnel.[11]

This provision mentions "cooperation" only with respect to "preserving order and discipline among United States military and naval personnel," and makes no reference to cooperation between Philippine and United States authorities in investigating offenses which occurred on the bases in which the offender and the offended were both Filipinos. In most such cases the United States authorities were willing to cooperate. In others, however, the United States was not willing to do so. One of these involved offenses committed against Filipino "intruders" by Philippine civilian security guards employed on the bases. Under the provisions of Article XIII the Philippines should have had the right to exercise jurisdiction in such cases.[12] In the absence of a specific provision calling for United States cooperation, however, the Philippines in most instances was not able to implement its right to exercise jurisdiction.

Only the provisions relative to criminal jurisdiction of the NATO SOFA which radically differed from those of the United States-Philippine agreement have been mentioned. Other lesser differences existed, but as will be seen in the following chapter, the radical differences were the basis of a majority of the problems which arose under the 1947 agreement.[13]

[11] This provision remains in effect under the 1965 agreement.

[12] The provisions of Article XIII refer only to members of the United States "armed forces" and not to members of its civilian component or dependents. Since Articles XI, XII, XVI, XVIII, and XXIII of the agreement mention employees and dependents separately from members of the armed (or military) forces, it seems appropriate to conclude that the term "armed forces," as used in Article XIII, is not meant to include members of the civilian component or dependents. Thus even if the Filipino guards were considered to be members of the United States civilian component, the Philippine authorities would legally have jurisdiction.

[13] All of the provisions of the NATO SOFA which have been presented also have been included in the United States-Japanese status of forces agreement since 1953. The status of

The Constitutional Test

One of the most controversial provisions of the 1947 agreement, that which gave the United States the right to exercise jurisdiction over Filipinos who committed criminal offenses on the bases, became the subject of the Philippine constitutional test of the validity of the agreement. The first case in which the constitutionality of the agreement came under attack involved Miquiabas, a Filipino citizen and civilian employee of the United States military, who was charged with "disposing in the Port of Manila Area of things belonging to the United States Army, in violation of the 94th Article of War of the United States."[14] Since the alleged offense had been committed within a temporary installation of the United States Army, the military authorities classified it as an on-base offense and claimed jurisdiction under the provisions of Article XIII, paragraph 1(a) of the 1947 bases agreement. Miquiabas was tried by court-martial, found guilty, and sentenced to fifteen years imprisonment. Shortly thereafter he sought habeas corpus relief from the Philippine Supreme Court on the grounds that the Port of Manila Area was not a base within the meaning of the agreement and even if it were, his trial by a foreign court-martial, as was provided in the agreement, was a violation of his constitutional rights.

The Supreme Court held that the offense was not committed on a base within the meaning of the agreement and, therefore, Article XIII, paragraph 1(a) was inapplicable.[15] The Court further pointed out that

United States forces in Japan has been under three different agreements since the security treaty [Signed at San Francisco September 8, 1951, ratifications exchanged April 28, 1952; 3 *UST* 3329; *TIAS* 2491] entered into force. For the interim arrangements before the 1953 United States-Japanese agreement came into effect, during which time the United States had exclusive jurisdiction over its personnel, see Article XVII of the Administrative Agreement under Article III of the Security Treaty, and Exchange of Notes, signed at Tokyo February 28, 1952, entered into force April 28, 1952; 3 *UST* 3341; *TIAS* 2492. The 1953 agreement amended Article XVII so as to follow the basic guidelines of the NATO SOFA. See Protocol to Amend Article XVII of the Administrative Agreement... Signed at Tokyo September 29, 1953; entered into force October 29, 1953. 4 *UST* 1846; *TIAS* 2848. When the new security treaty [Signed at Washington January 19, 1960; 11 *UST* 1632; *TIAS* 4509] entered into force on June 23, 1960, a new agreement regarding the status of United States forces in Japan also came into effect. See Article XVII of Agreement under Article VI of the Treaty of Mutual Cooperation and Security... Signed at Washington January 19, 1960; entered into force June 23, 1960. 11 *UST* 1652; *TIAS* 4510. Under this agreement, however, the criminal jurisdictional arrangements remained the same as under the 1953 agreement, with the NATO SOFA arrangements continuing to serve as guideposts. In the Philippines, although the NATO SOFA jurisdictional provisions were referred to most often as the standard for revising the United States-Philippine agreement, the fact that Japan, a former enemy of the United States, was treated as more of an equal by the United States than was the Philippines was particularly irritating to the Filipinos.

[14] *Miquiabas* v. *Commanding General*, 80 Phil. 262 (1948).

[15] *Ibid.*, pp. 266–268.

the accused was not a member of the armed forces within the meaning of Article XIII, 1(b), and thus the judgment of the court-martial was "null and void for lack of jurisdiction." The petitioner was ordered released "without prejudice to any criminal action which may be instituted in the proper courts of the Philippines."[16]

Since Miquiabas was released on the grounds that the Port of Manila Area was not a base within the meaning of the agreement, it was not necessary for the Court to consider the constitutionality of the agreement. In *obiter dictum*, however, Justice Moran, for the Court, noted:

> It may be stated as a general rule that the Philippines, being a sovereign nation, has jurisdiction over all offenses committed within its territory, but it may, by treaty or by agreement, consent that the United States or any other foreign nation, shall exercise jurisdiction over certain offenses committed within certain portions of said territory.[17]

The actual constitutional test came a short time later when the Philippine Supreme Court was asked to rule on another habeas corpus action, quite similar to that of the *Miquiabas* case. Dizon, the petitioner, was a Filipino civilian employee of the United States military, who allegedly had committed an offense at Philrycom Engineer Depot, United States Army, Quezon City.[18] He was prosecuted and convicted by a general court-martial of the United States Army and given five years at hard labor. As in the *Miquiabas* case, the petitioner argued that the particular area was not a base in the meaning of the 1947 agreement, and even if it were, the provisions of Article XIII allowing United States court-martial jurisdiction over Philippine citizens were unconstitutional because they deprived the "Philippine courts of the jurisdiction over all offenses exclusively vested in them by Article VIII, section 1, of the [Philippine] Constitution," and violated "section 1 of Article II of the Constitution guaranteeing to every person in the Philippines due process and equal protection of the law."[19]

The Court first ruled that the particular military installation involved was covered by the provisions of the bases agreement and, therefore, Article XIII of the agreement was applicable. With respect to the question of the constitutionality of the agreement the Court pointed out that in the *Raquiza* case[20] and in the *Tubb* case[21] the Court had

[16] *Ibid.*, pp. 268–270.
[17] *Ibid.*, p. 264. Although the decision of the Court was concurred in by all members of the Court, Justice Perfecto wrote a separate opinion. Specifically, he did not agree with Justice Moran's statement.
[18] *Dizon* v. *Commanding General*, 81 Phil. 286 (1948).
[19] *Ibid.*, pp. 289–290.
[20] *Raquiza* v. *Bradford*, 75 Phil. 50 (1945).
[21] *Tubb and Tedrow* v. *Griess*, 78 Phil. 249 (1947).

applied the well-settled principle of International Law that a foreign army allowed to march through a friendly country or to be stationed in it, by permission of its government or sovereign, is exempt from the civil and criminal jurisdiction of the place.[22]

The Court further stated that such exemption is not

an unconstitutional diminution or deprivation of the jurisdiction of the Philippine courts... because by virtue of section 3 of Article II of the Constitution, the generally accepted principles of international law have been adopted as part of the law of the Nation. In like manner, there would not be an unconstitutional derogation of the jurisdiction of the local courts if we were to recognize the immunities of foreign sovereigns and ministers...[23]

The Court continued by pointing out that the 1947 agreement gave the United States "express permission to establish military bases on certain portions of the Philippine territory and to exercise jurisdiction over certain offenses." The rights granted under the agreement, the Court stated "are no less than those conceded by the rule of international law to 'a foreign army allowed to march through a friendly country...'" The jurisdiction granted to the United States by the terms of the agreement

may be wider than what is recognized by international law [in that in some cases the United States has jurisdiction over Filipinos], but the fact remains that the lesser right is fundamentally as much a diminution of the jurisdiction of the Philippine courts as the greater right.[24]

Thus the provision of Article VIII, section 1 of the Philippine Constitution which states that "the judicial power shall be vested in one Supreme Court and in such inferior courts as may be established by law" was not an absolute prohibition against trials conducted in accordance with international agreements.

The Court further stated that the bases granted to the United States were granted legally under the Tydings-McDuffie Act of 1934, Joint Resolution Number 93 of 1944, and the presidential proclamation of Philippine independence in July 1946. If the bases could be "validly granted to the United States under the Constitution," the Court pointed out, "there is no plausible reason why the lesser attribute of jurisdiction cannot be waived..." The Court concluded its argument by stating:

Jurisdiction being validly waived in favor of the United States under the agreement in question, it follows that petitioner's contention regarding alleged denial of due process and equal protection of the law becomes unfounded.[25]

[22] *Dizon* v. *Commanding General*, 81 Phil. 286, 291 (1948).
[23] *Ibid.*
[24] *Ibid.*, p. 294.
[25] *Ibid.*, pp. 293–294.

A vigorous and strongly worded dissent was given by Justice Perfecto who supported Dizon's contention, holding that the agreement was unconstitutional in that it denied due process and equal protection of the laws to Filipinos subjected to the jurisdiction of United States courts-martial proceedings. As he had stated a few months earlier in the *Miquiabas* case:

> The Bill of Rights has been embodied in the Constitution for the protection of all human beings within the territorial jurisdiction of the Philippines. All persons covered by the waivers made in the agreement, whether Americans or Filipinos, whether citizens or aliens, are denied the constitutional guarantee of the equal protection of the law. Their fundamental rights are safeguarded by the Constitution, and the agreement places them outside the Constitution.
>
> [My] conclusion is, therefore, that the agreement in question, so far as it stipulates waiver of the jurisdiction of our courts of justice on the class of persons mentioned therein, is null and void, being in open conflict with clear provisions of our fundamental law.[26]

In his dissent in the *Dizon* case Justice Perfecto also pointed out that the Court never had demonstrated that the exemption of military forces from the jurisdiction of a friendly foreign country was a generally accepted principle of international law. An attempt to find such a general principle, he maintained, would be futile. In a ringing conclusion, he attacked both the Philippine government and the United States government by stating:

> This Supreme Court has the power to stop the rampage of constitutional breaches in which other agencies of our government are indulging in a servile attitude of complaisance to former masters who are bent on keeping in their hands the strings, the chains, and the whip of unquestioned command.[27]

Justice Perfecto's critique notwithstanding, the agreement of 1947 successfully survived the constitutional challenge.[28]

[26] *Miquiabas* v. *Commanding General*, 80 Phil. 262, 271 (1948). This concurring opinion of Perfecto seems to deny United States military authorities the right to exercise jurisdiction even over United States military personnel. This may be an exaggeration on his part, but it does appear that he had an argument at least insofar as Filipinos themselves were concerned. Several years after the *Miquiabas* and *Dizon* cases, the United States Supreme Court held that civilian employees of the United States armed forces serving overseas in times of peace and charged with an offense there, cannot constitutionally be deprived of the protections of Article III and the Fifth and Sixth Amendments of the United States Constitution. See below, pp. 104–105. As Ebb has noted, this raised the interesting possibility that the United States Constitution itself prohibits the trial of Filipino civilian employees by United States courts-martial. This question, however, has never been before the Supreme Court. See Lawrence F. Ebb, *International Business* (St. Paul, Minn.: West Publishing Co., 1964), p. 16.

[27] *Dizon* v. *Commanding General*, 81 Phil. 286, 302 (1948).

[28] In a constitutional test in Japan an even more basic question, the constitutionality of the stationing of United States forces in Japan, was decided in favor of the United States in the *Sunakawa* case. For an extended commentary on this case, see Cho. "Jurisdiction over Foreign Forces in Japan," pp. 242–274.

Continuity in Jurisdictional Arrangements

A comparison of the criminal jurisdictional provisions of the 1947 agreement with the provisions of the earlier arrangements reveals a continuation of the basic arrangements which had been established in the pre-independence period. Perhaps this continuity has not received proper emphasis. Historical treatments of this subject usually begin with discussions of the Hare-Hawes-Cutting Act of 1933 and the Tydings-McDuffie Act of 1934, and proceed immediately from these acts to Joint Resolution 93 of 1944. Such limited accounts of the historical background of the provisions for the retention of the bases apparently have contributed to erroneous reports of the jurisdictional provisions. For the most part this has been the result of a too literal interpretation of the statutes, indicating that the bases always were excluded from the jurisdiction of the civil authorities. Meyer, in fact, stated that the military reservations had been excluded from the jurisdiction of the civil authorities since the passage of the Jones Act in 1916.[29] As has been pointed out in Chapter I, however, it was not until 1938 that the criminal jurisdictional arrangements changed from a civil orientation to a military orientation.

The criminal jurisdictional provisions of the 1947 agreement were in many respects quite similar to the arrangements established by Executive Order Number 151 of 1938, thus indicating that the relationship between the civil and military authorities during the period before independence later was reflected in the relationship between an independent Philippines and the United States. Since the 1947 agreement was signed shortly after the granting of Philippine independence, one might have expected its criminal jurisdictional arrangements to reflect the proud position of a newly independent nation. That this was not the case was due, at least in part, to the fact that Philippine independence was not granted under the threat of a rising tide of nationalism and revolutionary activity, but rather on the basis of a prearranged schedule.

In addition, World War II had placed the Filipinos in a difficult position to bargain with the United States. A majority of Philippine leaders agreed that Philippine security had to be protected by the United States, and therefore the United States bases in the Philippines had to be retained. Thus it was not the existence of the bases per se that presented problems, but rather the role and status of these bases,

[29] Meyer, p. 25.

a substantial part of which involved criminal jurisdiction. Necessity coupled with a background in the Philippines of military-oriented criminal jurisdictional arrangements apparently facilitated Philippine acceptance of the criminal jurisdictional arrangements of the 1947 agreement.

CHAPTER IV

CRIMINAL JURISDICTIONAL PROBLEMS UNDER THE 1947 BASES AGREEMENT

Initial Philippine reaction to the criminal jurisdictional provisions of the 1947 agreement was favorable. As the Filipinos gained confidence in the United States promises to protect their security and as their interest in sovereignty developed, they viewed these provisions from a changing perspective. Problems regarding criminal jurisdiction which arose between the United States military authorities and the Philippine authorities began to attract increasing attention and to generate considerable dissatisfaction. This was particularly true after the NATO Status of Forces Agreement (SOFA)[1] and the United States-Japanese agreement[2] came into effect in 1953. The Philippine press was influential in stimulating public interest by contrasting the Philippine agreement with other agreements, exposing problem areas, and reporting relevant cases. A majority of these cases seem to fall into five general categories: (1) Philippine prosecution of United States personnel for off-base offenses; (2) enforcement of Philippine laws on the bases; (3) offenses by United States personnel against Filipinos on the bases; (4) exercise of jurisdiction over Filipinos by the United States; and (5) killing and injury of Filipinos by security guards on the bases. This chapter will deal with each of these areas in some detail and attempt to show how each contributed to mounting demands by the Philippine authorities for revision of the criminal jurisdictional arrangements of the 1947 agreement.

Philippine Prosecution of United States Personnel for Off-Base Offenses

The provisions of Article XIII, paragraphs 1, 2, and 4, of the 1947 agreement stated that the Philippines had the right to exercise jurisdiction over "all offenses committed outside the bases by any member

[1] NATO SOFA. Cited above, chap. iii, note 8.

[2] Protocol to Amend Article XVII of the Administrative Agreement... Cited above, chap. iii, note 13.

of the armed forces of the United States," except in cases in which (a) "the offended party is also a member of the armed forces of the United States," (b) the offense is "against the security of the United States," (c) the offense is committed during the "actual performance of a specific military duty," and (d) the offense is committed "during a period of national emergency."[3]

Under these provisions the number of cases of United States personnel subject to Philippine jurisdiction fluctuated radically from year to year.[4] As can be seen in the Table below, records beginning in January 1954 indicate that a maximum of 182 cases occurred in 1958, and a minimum of 47 in 1956. The percentage of these cases actually tried also fluctuated, from a high of 20% in 1963 to a low of 1% in 1954. Although the highest percentages of cases tried occurred in 1963 and 1964, no consistently increasing trend is apparent.

The rate of waiver of jurisdiction by the Philippines was far lower than it was for other countries with which the United States has status of forces agreements. For all of the NATO countries combined the yearly waiver rate stayed consistently around 60–65%.[5] Under the United States-Philippine agreement the waiver rate was high for the first three years reported, but dropped to virtually nothing after 1956. From 1961–1964 there were only four waivers out of 344 cases or slightly over one percent.

In sharp contrast to the low percentage of cases waived by the Philippines was the high percentage of cases in which the charges were dropped. This high percentage of charges dropped accounted for the low percentage of cases actually tried by the Philippines. From 1961–1964 the rate of charges dropped averaged 90% which is ex-

[3] See above, pp. 37–38.

[4] One-third of the 1,030 cases reported from 1954 through 1964 were traffic violations, but a substantial number involved more serious offenses. The cases fall into twelve categories. These categories (as used by the Department of Defense) and the percentage of cases in each are as follows: murder, less than .5%; rape, 3%; manslaughter (including negligent homicide), 3%; robbery, larceny and related offenses, 9%; burglary and related offenses, 1%; forgery and related offenses, less than .5%; aggravated assault, 5%; simple assault, 18%; offenses against economic control laws, 1%; traffic offenses (including drunken and reckless driving and fleeing scene of accident), 34%; disorderly conduct, drunkeness, breach of peace, etc., 15%; others, 10%. Computed from U.S. Department of Defense, *OCS Form 782*, 1954–1955; and *JAG Form 66*, 1956–1964, inclusive.

[5] Since 1955 a Subcommittee of the Committee on Armed Services of the Senate has held yearly hearings on the operation of Article VII of the NATO SOFA and the similar provisions of other status of forces agreements. This datum is drawn from these hearings. See U.S., Congress, Senate, Subcommittee of the Committee on Armed Services, *Hearings, Operation of Article VII, NATO Status of Forces Treaty*, 84th Cong., 1st Sess., 1955–89th Cong., 1st Sess., 1965. Hereafter, the *Hearings* will be referred to as *Operation Hearings* with the appropriate year.

TABLE

Summary of Exercise of Criminal Jurisdiction by Philippine Courts over United States Personnel, 1954–1964, Inclusive[a]

Year[b]	New Cases	Waived	% Waived[c]	Dropped	% Dropped[c]	Pending	Tried	% Tried[c]	Convicted	% Convicted[d]	Fined Only	Confined
1954	156	123	79	28	18	4	1	1	0	0	0	0
1955	99	41	47	40	46	16	4	5	2	0	2	0
1956	47	22	41	22	41	9	10	19	1	10	0	1
1957	49	1	2	38	93	17	2	5	2	100	2	0
1958	182	1	1	178	96	13	6	3	4	67	3	1
1959	82	1	1	86	97	7	2	2	1	50	0	1
1960	72	1	2	49	91	27	2	4	1	0	0	1
1961	60	2	3	66	93	16	3	4	1	33	0	1
1962	85	0	0	77	95	20	4	5	2	50	1	1
1963	67	2	3	50	77	22	13	20	4	31	4	0
1964	132	0	0	104	89	37	13	11	10	77	9	1

[a] Calculated from: U.S. Department of Defense, *OCS Form 782*, 1954–1955; and *JAG Form 66*, 1956–1964, inclusive.

[b] The reporting period for 1954 is from January 1, 1954 to November 30, 1954. All other reporting years are from December 1 of the previous year to November 30 of the listed year, i.e., the year listed 1955 covers the period from December 1, 1954 to November 30, 1955.

[c] For purposes of calculation the total number of cases was taken to be the new cases plus cases held over from the previous reporting year minus the pending cases.

[d] Percentage is computed from the number of cases tried.

ceedingly high compared with the figures for other countries with which the United States has status of forces agreements.[6] The primary reason for this high rate of cases in which charges were dropped was that in the Philippines both the criminal and the civil aspects of a particular case are handled at the same time. As an official of the United States Department of the Navy explained, the procedure in a typical case in which the Philippines had the right to exercise jurisdiction was as follows:

> The complainant would notify the fiscal of the alleged offense and the fiscal would charge the accused. [In the Philippines] both the civil and criminal aspects of an incident are determined at the same trial. Before trial, the complainant and the accused would reach a financial settlement and the complainant would withdraw the complaint. The Philippine court would then dismiss the charge, whereupon naval authorities would take whatever disciplinary action was appropriate...[7]

[6] For all of the countries with which the United States has status of forces agreements the yearly dropped rate has usually been under 5%. See *Operation Hearings 1955–Operation Hearings 1965.*

[7] Personal letter from Captain Geoffrey E. Carlisle, Director, International Law Division, Department of the Navy, dated March 11, 1966. Also, personal letter from Commander W. J. Davis, Legal Officer, United States Naval Station, Sangley Point, dated April 11, 1966.

Because of this procedure almost all cases which came to trial in the Philippines were ones in which there was no injury to person or property.[8] An example of such a case is the following. On June 26, 1962, three sailors were accused of possessing opium at Olongapo, Zambales. Court proceedings at the Court of First Instance at Zambales took place on October 16, November 7, and November 15, 1962. The trial was completed on March 5, 1963, with the court acquitting two of the sailors and finding the third guilty. The latter was sentenced to a fine of three-hundred pesos and four months confinement. This conviction was appealed to the Court of Appeals, where the findings and the sentence were confirmed. Confinement began on September 3, 1965, but the sailor was released on September 8, "having been credited with the time spent in Navy custody since 26 June, 1962." Nine days later, however, "he was returned to Philippine authorities to serve the unexpired portion of this sentence pursuant to an order from the Court of First Instance to the effect that the credit was erroneous and the release premature."[9]

While the latter part of this case—pertaining to the confinement procedure—may have been unusual, the length of time involved in processing the case was not that unusual. It was quite typical of the slow judicial process found in the Philippines, which was the major complaint of the United States military authorities. Some of the complications which resulted from such a slow process were exemplified even more clearly in a case reported by a Clark Field official:

> In one case one of our airmen remained in the Republic of the Philippines for a period of four years pending the final disposition of his criminal case. At the time that he departed the Republic of the Philippines he was two and a half years beyond his normal rotation date. He did not serve any time in jail, and all the time was spent in the preliminary investigation, trial and appeal.[10]

Although United States military authorities voiced objections to the slow judicial process, they made no complaints about the percentage of those tried who were convicted or the type of punishments administered. The rate of convictions stayed fairly consistently between one-third and one-half of the cases tried. For the last four years reported the average yearly rate of convictions was 48%. Insofar as the United States military authorities were concerned, this did not appear objectionable.[11]

[8] Personal letter, Captain Carlisle, dated March 11, 1966.

[9] *Ibid.*

[10] Personal letter, Captain Richard J. Hackett, Director of International Law, Clark Air Base, dated April 14, 1966.

[11] For all of the countries with which the United States has status of forces agreements the

The same was true with respect to the type of punishment administered to those convicted. Few cases involved confinement, the majority requiring payment of fines only. Of the seventeen convictions for the 1961–1964 period, only three were punished by confinement, all for relatively short periods. The other fourteen convictions drew fines.

It appears, then, that the United States military authorities met no major problems relative to the trial of United States personnel by Philippine authorities with the exception of the slow judicial process. The Assistant Judge Advocate General of the Army informed a Senate subcommittee that the Army Commander had reported no "adverse effect" upon the "accomplishment of his mission or on the morale and discipline of the Army in the Philippines" because of the jurisdictional arrangements.[12] The Navy Commander in the Philippines went even further, reportedly stating that the "exercise of jurisdiction by Philippine authorities over our personnel has favorably affected the morale and discipline of our forces."[13] In particular, he noted, the "posed threat of arrest and conviction by Philippine courts with possible imprisonment in a Philippine jail contributes to good discipline."[14]

There are indications that many Philippine authorities also were fairly well satisfied with the trial of United States personnel by Philippine courts at least through 1956. As Locsin stated in late October 1956:

> The Philippine government, it may be said right here and now, finds nothing wrong with the situation outside U.S. bases. It is the situation inside the bases that is the subject of controversy between the two nations.[15]

This view is confirmed, at least in part, by an article published after the collapse of the Pelaez-Bendetsen talks in 1956. In this article, Undersecretary of Justice Barrera, in reporting on the then defunct talks, stated:

> Because jurisdiction over offenses committed outside the bases [by United States personnel] has not raised substantial and compelling issues, we may focus and confine our attention to the provisions on jurisdiction over offenses committed inside the bases.[16]

lowest yearly conviction rate was 94% in 1956. See *Operation Hearings 1957*, p. 14. A comparative study of conviction rates for the year 1957 reveals that for all trials before United States district courts the conviction rate was 96%; for all trials by general courts-martial, 95%; for all trials of United States personnel by foreign courts, 94%; and for all trials of United States personnel by the NATO SOFA countries combined the conviction rate was 93%. See *Operation Hearings 1958*, p. 59. As the Table of the present study indicates, the only year in which the Philippine conviction rate was this high was in 1957.

[12] *Operation Hearings 1955*, p. 37.

[13] *Ibid.*

[14] *Operation Hearings 1956*, p. 29.

[15] Teodore M. Locsin, *Free Press*, October 27, 1956, p. 2.

[16] Jesus G. Barrera, "The Constitution and the Military Bases Agreement," 1957 *Decision*

Since Barrera had been the chairman of the subcommittee handling the problem of jurisdiction during the 1956 talks, it seems reasonable to assume that the Philippine delegation did not view the question of jurisdiction over United States personnel for offenses committed off base as one of central concern.

Nevertheless, even before the talks began, developments were occurring which later led to a major complaint by the Philippines concerning off-base offenses. One indication of dissatisfaction was given by the Mayor of Manila in 1955. Until July of that year the Manila "courts did not take cognizance of cases involving American military personnel."[17] At that time, however, Mayor Lacson announced in his weekly radio broadcast:

> I am serving notice to American authorities in the Philippines that from now on every member of the United States Armed Forces who gets in trouble in the city of Manila, is not going to be bundled quietly to the Port area and turned over to the American Provost Marshall. He is going to be booked and thrown into the city jail and he will be prosecuted and tried under the laws of the Philippine Republic.[18]

In this same month Undersecretary of Justice Barrera, in commenting on the Curtis J. Willis case, a case in which a United States airman was accused of mauling a Filipino in Angeles City, Pampanga, stated that the civil courts should not waive jurisdiction to the Clark Field authorities because he believed that Willis would be "shipped out."[19] The specific basis for Barrera's belief is not known, but perhaps similar cases earlier had seen United States personnel shipped out of the Philippines without trial (either civil or military) or punishment. In any event, the problem of Philippine prosecution of United States personnel attracted increasing attention and came into sharp focus in the George E. Roe case.

In Cavite City on January 1, 1956, the car of George E. Roe, a seaman in the United States Navy, struck a forty-year old laundry woman, Rosario Ortiz, throwing her in front of the car of a United States civilian, Chester Hoff.[20] Both Roe and Hoff were detained by the local

Law Journal 643, 647 (1957). Valeros made the *same* statement in 1961, after spending seven pages condemning the United States military authorities for their actions in the Roe case—a case involving an off-base offense. See Antonio Valeros, "Jurisdiction of Philippine Courts Over Personnel of the United States Military Reservations in the Philippines," 4 *University of the East Law Journal* 18, 31 (1961).

[17] Tanjuakio, p. 611.

[18] *Manila Chronicle*, July 28, 1955, p. 2, as cited in Tanjuakio, p. 611.

[19] *Manila Times*, July 26, 1955, p. 1.

[20] On the same day Roy Cook of the United States Navy was involved in an automobile accident in Pasay City. Although charged in connection with the accident, Cook was transferred to Europe in June 1956. See *Manila Times*, July 27, 1957, p. 1; and Pablo B. Badong, "Philippine Jurisdiction Over the George E. Roe Case," 32 *Philippine Law Journal* 403, 403 (1957). This case, however, received little publicity.

authorities. Hoff later was released, and Roe was turned over to Sangley Point naval authorities while an investigation was conducted in accordance with Article XIII, paragraph 5, of the 1947 bases agreement. A complaint was formally filed with the Manila fiscal's office on January 12, 1956, accusing Roe of causing physical injuries through reckless driving. Preliminary investigations were conducted on February 28, March 27, and May 22, 1956. Roe appeared only once during the preliminary hearings but was represented by counsel from the United States Navy legal staff at the other hearings. When interviewed later Roe stated that he "went down to the Manila police station once. I got down there and then they said they didn't need me."[21]

On November 26, almost eleven months after the accident, an order for the arrest of Roe was referred to the Commanding Officer, United States Naval Station, Sangley Point.[22] Meanwhile Roe had been shipped back to the United States and discharged.[23] The Sangley Point naval authorities said that Roe's demobilization was a mistake, but nothing could be done to correct it.[24]

In the months that followed, the Roe case attracted considerable attention, receiving substantial coverage in the Philippine press and being discussed at length in two articles in major law journals.[25] Eventually the case became the subject of talks between the United States and the Philippines and occasioned a formal protest by the Philippine Foreign Office to the United States Embassay in the Philippines. This protest stated:

> It has been noted that this is not the first time that members of the armed forces of the United States who have been accused before the Philippine courts for one crime or another have been able to avoid trial and thereby defeat the ends of justice by seeking transfers from the United States military authorities to other places beyond the reach of the jurisdiction of the Philippine courts.[26]

The question of whether or not Roe should have been returned to the Philippines was considered by Badong in his article in the *Philippine Law Journal*. He noted that according to some authorities on international law the United States was not obligated legally to surrender Roe to the Philippine authorities because there was no extradition

[21] As quoted in the *Manila Times*, July 3, 1957, p. 8.
[22] See Badong, pp. 403–404.
[23] See *Manila Times*, July 27, 1957, p. 1.
[24] See Badong, p. 404; and Valeros, p. 25.
[25] See *Manila Daily Bulletin*, July 2, 1957, p. 15; *Manila Daily Bulletin*, July 3, 1957, p. 23; *Manila Times*, July 3, 1957, p. 8; *Manila Chronicle*, July 5, 1957, p. 22; *Manila Times*, July 27, 1957, p. 1; Badong, pp. 403–410; and Valeros, pp. 18–36.
[26] As quoted in Taylor, p. 237.

treaty between the United States and the Philippines.[27] Badong pointed out that these authorities had overlooked the "highly material fact" that the case was governed by the agreement of 1947. Since the offense was not committed while Roe was in the performance of a specific duty or during a national emergency, Badong argued that the Philippines had jurisdiction under paragraph 2 of Article XIII. The United States, he maintained, was obligated under international law to fulfill her treaty commitment. Even though Roe was now demobilized and the United States Navy had no control over him, Badong held that the agreement was between the United States and the Philippines, not between the United States Navy and the Philippines. In private international law, he stated, it is an accepted rule "that the applicable law in cases of offenses committed by foreigners in the territory of a State is the... law of the place where the offense was committed." Roe's case was a violation of Philippine law and hence Philippine law should be applied. Badong then noted that under Philippine law, when a serviceman who commits an offense while in service is discharged, no bar is present to prevent a trial for the offense.[28] If this rule were applied, he pointed out, Roe's demobilization was immaterial to the case. Citing the United States ruling in the *Girard* case, Badong argued that there is no question that the United States could surrender Roe under the Constitution of the United States.[29]

Baldwin, opposing the position taken by Badong, set forth several important points. First he noted that the eleven months delay between the time of the incident and the order of arrest in the Roe case lacked "elemental fairness," even if the accused were still subject to military law. As he stated:

> Whether or not the accused remains subject to military law, there is something incongruous about returning a man to a country for a minor criminal trial almost a year after the offense. In the Roe case criminal sanctions, if warranted, should have been imposed promptly and without an eleven months delay. The obligation of promptness on the authorities of the receiving state is of particular importance when the alleged offender is in military service, thousands of miles from his home. To authorize a substantial delay in the return of the person to his home or to require a return of the offender to the demanding country, a serious case should be presented.

[27] Badong did not make the point, but even President Garcia, although pledging the use of Philippine diplomatic and legal agencies to attempt to get Roe back, stated that only an extradition treaty could prevent such cases in the future. Garcia, at the time, stated that he was taking steps to revive the extradition treaty talks which broke off in 1948. 53 *Off. Gaz.* ccclii–cccliii (1957). As to the necessity of an extradition treaty to have a case such as Roe's handled by the Philippine authorities, see also the statement by Philippine Senator Fernandez, as quoted in Napoleon G. Rama, *Free Press*, January 9, 1965, p. 72.

[28] See *De La Paz* v. *CDR*, 52 *Off. Gaz.* 3037 (1956).

[29] Badong, pp. 404–408. For the *Girard* case, see *Wilson* v. *Girard*, 354 U.S. 524 (1957).

This is simply a matter of elemental fairness. If promptness is not observed, the principal objective of the status of forces agreements, the proper administration of criminal justice, is not fulfilled.[30]

Thus, Baldwin maintained that if the Philippines had taken prompt action in the Roe case the problem would not have arisen.[31] He went on to say that this was recognized by France in relation to the NATO SOFA when the Minister of Justice "instructed the *procureurs generaux* to take prompt action in the event of the prosection of a member of the armed forces."[32]

Baldwin also maintained that Badong's contention that the United States should return Roe even if he were no longer in the service "does not have merit." It is well established "as a matter of United States law," he stated, "that release from military service will confer jurisdictional immunity from a trial by court-martial."[33] He further added that each of the status of forces agreements takes as a point of departure that "the law of the military forces determine membership in that force, and that the capacity of a military force to control its members is determined by municipal law." Therefore, he argued, "if municipal law does not permit the United States to exercise authority over a person, then the receiving state in a status of forces situation cannot claim a breach of the agreement."[34]

Baldwin's point that under United States law a release from military service confers jurisdictional immunity from a trial by court-martial is well taken, as is his point that the law of the military forces determines membership in that force. Badong's error came from trying to compare the *Girard* case, in which the accused was still in the military service, with the Roe case, in which the accused had been discharged. Since Roe was no longer subject to military law and the Philippines had no extradiction treaty with the United States, there seems to be no question that Roe could not have been returned to the Philippines under existing United States law.[35]

[30] Gordon B. Baldwin, "Jurisdiction and the American Soldier: The Adventures of Girard," 1958 *Wisconsin Law Review* 52, 90 (1958).

[31] On being interviewed in Clio, Michigan after his discharge, Roe stated that he did not know he had been indicted. "They questioned me," he stated, "and hadn't decided anything when I left." *Manila Times*, July 3, 1957, p. 8.

[32] Baldwin, p. 91. See Sec. V, Circular from French Minister of Justice to the Procureurs Generaux, titled: "Allied Forces Stationed in France by Virtue of the North Atlantic Treaty"; translated by Headquarters, United States Army, Europe Communications Zone, August 1953, as cited in *ibid.*

[33] See *United States ex rel. Toth* v. *Quarles*, 350 U.S. 11 (1955).

[34] Baldwin, pp. 90–91.

[35] As has been noted by the United States Supreme Court, international law recognizes no right to extradition apart from a treaty. See *Factor* v. *Laubenheimer*, 290 U.S. 276 (1933).

Whereas under the bases agreement the United States was obligated to produce Roe for trial, the Philippines, one would presume, was obligated to render a prompt trial.[36] As Baldwin noted, the latter is particularly important when a military man is thousands of miles from his home. This slow judicial process, however, has not been altered. The major mitigating aspect of this procedure is the fact that there are so few trials of United States personnel by the Philippine courts.

Whatever the legal questions involved in the Roe case, the case itself apparently made an impression on the United States military authorities in the Philippines. If transfer and/or discharge constituted the standard operating procedure prior to 1957,[37] it no longer did so after the Roe case. No similar case has been found, although several Philippine sources erroneously have compared another case to the Roe case.[38] This comparison was made by both the *Manila Times* and Valeros with respect to the Osborn case.

In this case, an American sailor, H. R. Osborn, was involved in a traffic accident on December 29, 1956, in which a sixty-year old farmer, Nicolas Bautista of Dasmariñas, Cavite, was seriously injured.[39] Osborn was discharged and shipped back to the United States on May 24, 1957. A criminal complaint was filed on June 27.[40] According to the *Manila Times* the late filing of the complaint was "obviously due to some oversight" on the part of Philippine authorities.[41] The Staff Legal Officer at Sangley Point Naval Station received a summons for Osborn on July 8. He returned the summons saying that this was the first he had heard of the case, and that Osborn had been discharged and sent home almost two months earlier.[42]

It is clear that the United States courts will not surrender any person to a foreign government unless such is specifically provided, even if a treaty exists. See *Valentine* v. *United States ex rel. Neidecker*, 299 U.S. 5 (1936); and *In re Lo Dolce*, 106 F. Supp. 455 (1953).

Although Roe could not have been returned to the Philippines under United States law, his removal from the Philippines may have constituted a breach of the 1947 agreement. The Philippines apparently did not press such a claim.

[36] Although the agreement of 1947 makes no reference to a "prompt trial" in cases in which the Philippines exercised jurisdiction over United States military personnel, such provisions are included in the Philippine Constitution at Article III, paragraph 17, where it is stated: "In all criminal prosecutions the accused... shall enjoy the right... to have a speedy and public trial..."

[37] No source indicated that Roe or any other military personnel were demobilized before their enlistment expired in order to avoid prosecution.

[38] There was, of course, the Cook case, but it apparently was "concluded" before the Roe case was "settled."

[39] Valeros, p. 24.

[40] *Manila Times*, August 1, 1957, p. 1.

[41] *Ibid.* It should be noted that no Philippine sources accepted the Sangley Point authorities' explanation that Roe's transfer and discharge had been a "mistake."

[42] *Ibid.*

The facts of the two cases made it quite clear that insofar as the responsibilities of the Navy were concerned the Osborne case was essentially different from the Roe case. In spite of this, the *Manila Times* claimed that they were similar. Valeros, either through oversight or misrepresentation, led one to believe that the naval authorities had been officially notified of the proceedings against Osborne and in spite of this had discharged him and sent him to the United States. As has been noted, however, the official proceedings had not begun when Osborne was discharged. It would appear that the United States military authorities in the Philippines were quite conscious of the possible ramifications of another Roe case and were careful to avoid such an occurrence.

Enforcement of Philippine Laws on the Bases

The 1947 agreement made no specific statement concerning the enforcement of Philippine laws on the bases granted to the United States. Nevertheless, this became one of the most important aspects of United States-Philippine relations relative to the bases. As the Philippine Supreme Court pointed out in the *Acierto* case:

> By the [1947 Bases] Agreement... the Philippine Government merely consents that the United States exercise jurisdiction in certain cases. This consent was given purely as a matter of comity, courtesy, or expediency. The Philippine Government has not abdicated its sovereignty over the bases as part of the Philippine territory or divested itself completely of jurisdiction over offenses committed therein. Under the terms of the treaty, the United States Government has prior or preferential but not exclusive jurisdiction of such offenses.[43]

This indicated that Philippine laws remained applicable on the bases granted to the United States. Yet, as the Supreme Court also noted, there were no Philippine law enforcement agencies located on the bases, with the result that what Philippine laws were enforced had to be enforced, at least initially, by the United States military authorities.[44] As would be expected, this type of arrangement led to numerous problems. For purposes of discussion the cases which resulted will be categorized according to the status of the offender. The first category will include offenses committed by Philippine nationals, not members of the United States armed forces, and the second will include offenses by United States military personnel, civilian employees, and their dependents.

[43] *People* v. *Acierto*, 49 *Off. Gaz.* 518, 524 (1953).
[44] See *Liwanag* v. *Hamill*, 52 *Off. Gaz.* 1396 (1956).

Apprehension and Prosecution of Philippine Nationals. Although the 1947 agreement did not mention the enforcement on the bases of Philippine laws, paragraph 1 (a) of Article XIII stated that the United States had jurisdiction over Filipinos for offenses committed on the bases which were not against other Filipinos or against Philippine national security. As will be seen below, the United States exercised this right infrequently and only in a certain class of cases prior to 1948 and did not exercise it at all after 1948.[45] Thus, although many of the offenses committed on the bases by Filipinos were violations of both United States and Philippine law, the United States in most such cases turned over the offenders to the Philippine authorities under the provisions of Article XIII, paragraph 3.[46]

The usual procedure for handling infractions of Philippine law committed on the bases by Filipinos was as follows. A Filipino national who was apprehended on the bases committing a violation of the law of the Republic of the Philippines initially was taken into custody by the base law enforcement personnel,[47] who gathered the appropriate evidence and drafted a criminal complaint (information) against the accused if there was sufficient evidence to "make a case." "The accused, along with the evidence, and the criminal complaint" was turned over to the appropriate local Philippine court.[48] At this stage, "a Filipino judge decided whether there was sufficient evidence against the accused to proceed with a preliminary investigation." If he found that there was sufficient evidence, a date for preliminary investigation was set. Such a preliminary investigation may have been "handled by the judge himself, or by the City or Provincial Fiscal's Office, depending on the court." There was no basic distinction between the procedure of apprehension by the base law enforcement personnel, when dealing with a major or a minor offense, except with regard to the steps taken to safeguard custody of the accused offender until he was delivered to the Philippine civil authorities, and with regard to the length of time a Philippine national could be held by the base authorities pending his investigation on criminal charges.[49]

[45] See below, pp. 67–70.

[46] See above, p. 38.

[47] Unless otherwise noted the following is drawn from: personal letter from Commander Davis, dated April 11, 1966; and personal letter from Captain Hackett, dated April 14, 1966.

[48] All such cases are handled by the regular municipal and provincial courts. At Angeles City, Pampanga, however, a regular court—the Municipal Court of Clark Field—has been established to handle Clark Field cases.

[49] "Under the laws of the Philippines, for: a) a light offense—there is a six hour period in which the information must be filed or the accused released; b) for less serious offenses—there is a nine hour period; and c) for serious offenses—there is an eighteen hour period."

Although this was the regular procedure it was not based on formal arrangements between the base authorities and the local Philippine authorities. As one United States military official noted:

> We do not have a formal arrangement with the local authorities in cases of a criminal nature [involving the apprehension and prosecution of accused Filipinos]. The offender is merely turned over to the local law enforcement agencies, who are also furnished with reports, etc.

The same authority, however, reported that he "attempts to keep a close personal liaison with local Fiscals to assure that cases we are particularly interested in do come to trial." It appears that although there were no "formal arrangements," there were more or less regularized procedures which were followed closely.

In the procedures involving the prosecution of Filipinos for alleged offenses on the bases numerous problems arose, many of which were worked out gradually over the years. A case which illustrated several of these problems was *Liwanag* v. *Hamill.*[50] In the *Liwanag* case the Assistant Base Provost Marshall at Clark Field, Major Hamill, had filed a complaint against Liwanag for having in his possession and control seventeen cartons of American cigarettes which had been imported free of tax and which were for the exclusive use of the United States military and naval forces in the Philippines. Such possession and control, without payment of the tax, the complaint stated, was in violation of section 174 of the National Internal Revenue Code of the Philippines. The complaint by Hamill was subscribed to and sworn before Judge Licup, the Justice of the Peace and a Philippine official at Clark Air Base.[51] Counsel for Liwanag attempted to quash the complaint in the Justice of the Peace Court, but this was denied by Judge Licup. Liwanag then filed a petition for prohibition with the Court of First Instance of Pampanga "alleging that Robert S. Hamill had no personal capacity to subscribe to the complaint and the Justice of the Peace Court, therefore, acquired no jurisdiction to conduct the preliminary investigation."[52] Liwanag's petition was predicated on the claim that Hamill was not an officer of the government of the Philippines and could not represent the plaintiff, the People of the Philippines, in a criminal case. The Court of First Instance agreed with Liwanag, holding that Hamill was "not a peace officer of the Republic

[50] *Liwanag* v. *Hamill,* 52 *Off. Gaz.* 1396 (1956).

[51] This official is no longer present on the base at Clark Air Base. Criminal complaints are now presented to the Municipal Court of Clark Field located at Angeles City, presided over at present by Judge Eloy D. David, who is appointed for life by the President of the Philippines.

[52] *Liwanag* v. *Hamill,* 52 *Off. Gaz.* 1396, 1396 (1956).

of the Philippines and, therefore, not authorized to file a complaint in accordance with section 2, Rule 100 of the Rules of Court."[53] From this decision Hamill appealed to the Supreme Court.

In an unanimous decision the Supreme Court, through Justice Labrador, first noted that the provost marshalls on military bases were peace officers and that "they have the powers and duties of chiefs of police in municipalities."[54] However, the Court continued by stating that the appeal was from a decision which said that provost marshalls were not peace officers of the Republic of the Philippines and consequently were not authorized to file complaints for violation of the Internal Revenue Code. This led the Court to a general discussion of the relationship between the civilian authorities of the Philippines and the military authorities of the United States with respect to criminal offenses committed on the bases. Under the agreement between the Philippines and the United States, the Court stated, the "laws of the Philippines continue to be in force in said bases except when otherwise agreed upon in the agreement." The Court noted that for the purpose of hearing cases on the bases justices of the peace were appointed by the President of the Philippines and held office on the bases. Besides these officers, however, there were no other officers of the Philippines who were appointed in the bases, "although agents of the Republic of the Philippines may have access in the bases to see that the laws of the Philippines are enforced." The Court pointed out: "To allow peace officers of said Republic to go therein and make arrests and institute prosecutions for violations of Philippine laws would certainly give occasion for conflicts of authority." Because of this possibility of conflicts of authority no provisions were made by the Philippines to appoint police officers in the bases. The Court held that in the absence of any Philippine law enforcement personnel the question of peace and order on the bases was the responsibility of peace officers of the United States, "the chief of whom is the provost marshall." The Court further stated that it would be "technical ceremony to allow a provost marshall to apprehend violators of Philippine laws and deny him the authority to prosecute such offenses before a Philippine court established inside the bases."[55] Thus the Court clearly upheld the right of the peace officers of the United States to arrest, apprehend, and prosecute violators of Philippine law for offense committed on the base.

[53] *Ibid.*, pp. 1396–1397.
[54] *Ibid.*, p. 1397.
[55] *Ibid.*, pp. 1397–1398.

Effectiveness of Procedure. As one United States military official stated, basically the present arrangements "are good working procedures between the two governments." He went on to say that the one major complaint of the United States authorities concerned the slow judicial process, the same complaint voiced with respect to the prosecution of United States personnel for off-base offenses. This was a problem, he noted,

> that is encountered in the prosecution of Philippine Nationals or in the defense of military or civilian dependents in Philippine courts... Preliminary investigations and or trials can last many years. Preliminary investigations and trials are different than back in the U.S. Trials and preliminary investigations are not heard... [to completion], but a case is called, a witness is examined, and the case is postponed until another day. Trials and preliminary investigations are handled in this piece meal fashion, and length of time between hearing dates may amount to a month or more.[56]

As another official noted, this slow judicial process became particularly important in the prosecution of Filipinos because "military witnesses sometimes leave before the case can be finally adjudicated."[57] Other than this complaint, however, the procedures appeared to be satisfactory.

One reason for the general success of the procedures may have been that in addition to formal prosecution by the Philippine authorities, the United States had another potent sanction. This was particularly true in cases involving the United States as the injured party, as in pilferage.[58] In such cases the United States could exercise powerful administrative sanctions. It was noted by one military official at Sangley Point Naval Base that "in virtually every case" involving pilferage by Philippine nationals, "the offender is barred from future access to U.S. Military Bases in the Philippines. He is thus deprived of an opportunity for employment with U.S. Government agencies in the Philippines."[59] Given the relatively high wages and privileges that Filipinos received for United States employment, it was likely that, especially with respect to those already employed by the United States, such potential administrative action substantially deterred criminal offenses. It has been noted, however, that administrative measures were not "particularly effective when a professional thief is involved."[60]

Procedures for United States Personnel. Almost all cases involving criminal

[56] Personal letter from Captain Hackett, dated April 14, 1966.

[57] Personal letter from Commander Davis, dated May 26, 1966.

[58] Apparently most of the offenses committed on the bases by Filipinos involved pilferage of United States property.

[59] Personal letter from Commander Davis, dated May 26, 1966.

[60] *Ibid.*

offenses on the bases by United States military personnel against Philippine law were also criminal offenses under the Uniform Code of Military Justice (U.C.M.J.).[61] Hence such cases almost always were handled through court-martial procedures. With respect to members of the civilian component and dependents, however, courts-martial have been without jurisdiction since 1960 when the United States Supreme Court declared that Congress does not have the power to subject civilians to court-martial jurisdiction in times of peace.[62] Thus, if a formal trial of a civilian for a serious criminal offense occurred in the Philippines after 1960, it would have been prosecuted before a Philippine court. This procedure, however, was put to little use. At Sangley Point Naval Base, for example, there was no such case. An official at that base stated that "inasmuch as we would retain our responsibilities for the individuals' welfare, etc. during the processing of the case, the simple expedients of discharge and removal from the Philippines are normally followed."[63] Thus, apparently administrative sanctions, which ranged from the denial of certain base privileges to discharge or removal from the Philippines, were extremely important in maintaining discipline of the civilian component and dependents.

In some instances, however, the United States military authorities brought criminal actions against American military and civilian personnel in Philippine courts for criminal offenses committed on the bases. An official at Clark Field reported:

> Actions brought by U.S. authorities against American military and civilian personnel do occur. In a recent case, U.S. authorities prosecuted an American citizen who cashed bogus checks in the Non-Commissioned Officers' Open Mess. He was convicted on 17 individual criminal cases filed in the Court of First Instance, and sentenced to seven years and to indemnify the NCO for the missing funds.[64]

Thus some of the United States military authorities used the sanctions of the Philippine legal system for criminal offenses by United States personnel which occurred on the bases. Apparently, all military authorities in the Philippines would have taken such actions if they felt that available administrative sanctions were not sufficient.[65]

[61] This is because of the general sweep of Article 134 of the Code. See below, chap. VI, note 15.

[62] See below, chap. VI, note 7.

[63] Personal letter from Commander Davis, dated April 11, 1966.

[64] Personal letter from Captain Hackett, dated April 14, 1966.

[65] In the new instructions for implementing the 1965 agreement the base commanders are directed to request waivers in cases in which the Philippines "may assume criminal jurisdiction over or take custody of dependents of United States military personnel, civilian personnel and their dependents" *only* when the base commander determines that he can take "suitable corrective action under existing administrative regulations..." See CINCPAC

Offenses by United States Personnel against Filipinos on the Bases

Under the 1947 agreement the United States was given jurisdiction over all offenses committed on the bases except those in which only Filipinos were involved and those which involved Philippine national security. Thus cases involving criminal actions by United States personnel against Filipinos came under the jurisdiction of the United States military authorities. Although the legal issues concerning this question were quite clear, such cases offered numerous possibilities for Philippine complaints as to the sufficiency of the 1947 agreement. One such case was that involving Walter Huggins.

Huggins, in April 1958, "stabbed to death a Filipina, Florenda Valdueza, in a bar on the American naval base in Olongapo, Zambales." It was reported that an American medical board examined Huggins, declared that he was "'unable to distinguish right from wrong,'" and sent him to Japan for further examination. The family of Valdueza asked for a record of the examination, but the naval authorities refused to make it available, presumably on the grounds that the United States had exclusive jurisdiction in the case. Secretary of Justice Barrera reportedly stated that in such cases the Philippines was absolutely "helpless" under the existing agreement.[66]

A similar case involved the killing of Rolando Cosca, a Filipino, in a bar at Olongapo. Cosca was hit with a chair and killed by a drunken United States sailor while the latter was in a fight with other United States sailors. As with the Huggins case, this case occurred on the base and therefore came under the jurisdiction of the United States military authorities.[67]

Cases like the Huggins case and the Cosca case not only created considerable friction but also led to the suggestion of hypothetical cases which became more of a rallying cry than the real cases. Locsin, for example, stated:

> A Filipina was stabbed to death by an American on an American base; the American was sent out of the country; the Philippine government could do nothing about it. A Filipina could be raped on a U.S. base, and again the Philippine government would be able to do nothing about it. A Filipino child could be run over by the wife of an American, whether a military man or a civilian employee, and the woman sent out of the country and never tried—What could the Philippine government do about it? Nothing. A Filipino could be killed—by a Chinese, on a U.S. base in the

Representative Philippines and Commander, U.S. Naval Forces Philippines, *CINCPACREP PHIL/COMNAVPHIL Instruction 5820.1B*, dated September 7, 1965, paragraph 12(a).

[66] Locsin, *Free Press*, December 20, 1958, p. 2.

[67] See Valeros, p. 23, and the *Manila Chronicle*, April 9, 1959, p. 1.

Philippines, and still the Philippine government would not be able to try the Chinese, or make sure that he was properly tried for the crime. The Philippine government would have no jurisdiction over the case.[68]

The Filipinos obviously were not satisfied with the jurisdictional arrangements dealing with this aspect of the problem.

Exercise of Jurisdiction over Filipinos by the United States

One of the most severely criticized aspects of the 1947 bases agreement was the provision of Article XIII, paragraph 1(a) which allowed the United States to exercise jurisdiction over Filipinos for on-base offenses (except in cases in which the offended party was also a Filipino or where the offense was against the security of the Philippines). Under this provision, as has been noted in Chapter III, the United States Army exercised jurisdiction over Miquiabas and Dizon, both of whom were employees of the army at the time of their alleged offenses. A later similar case was that involving Sengundo Acierto who was employed by the United States Army at Camp Rizal as a court-martial reporter on a piece-work basis.[69] In March 1948 the Army charged him with making false claims and receiving compensation for services not rendered. He was convicted by a general court-martial and sentenced to five years at hard labor. The reviewing authority, however, disapproved the sentence "upon the sole ground that this accused was not subject to military law and without prejudice to his trial before a proper tribunal."[70] As was later pointed out, this position was taken by the reviewing authority because Acierto due to his type of employment was not considered to be an employee of the Army within the meaning of United States military law.[71]

It should be noted that although the 1947 agreement gave the United States military authorities the right to exercise jurisdiction over a Filipino for an offense committed on a military base whether or not he was an employee, the United States at the time of the *Acierto* case had

[68] Locsin, *Free Press*, December 20, 1958, p. 2. See also Crispino de Castro, "U.S. Jurisdiction over Armed Forces in the Philippines," 7 *Far Eastern Law Review* 626, 642–643 (1959).

[69] See *People* v. *Acierto*, 49 *Off. Gaz.* 518; 92 Phil. 534 (1953). For the court-martial aspects of the case, see 92 Phil. 534, 535–540.

[70] As quoted in *ibid.*, p. 538. After this decision by the reviewing authority, the military authorities at Camp Rizal turned Acierto over to the Philippine authorities for prosecution in the Philippine courts. After conviction in the Municipal Court of Quezon City, Acierto appealed to the Supreme Court on a plea of double jeopardy. The conviction was upheld by the Court.

[71] *Amicus curiae* brief of the Staff Judge Advocate General of the Philippines Ryukus Command, as cited in *ibid.*, p. 540.

no forum under United States law to exercise jurisdiction unless the accused was employed by the United States armed forces. This situation changed, however, with the passage of the Uniform Code of Military Justice in 1950. Article 2, paragraph 12, of the Code expanded United States jurisdiction to include

> all persons within an area leased or otherwise reserved or acquired for the use of the United States which is under the control of the Secretary of a Department and which is without the continental limits of the United States...[72]

Thus from 1950 until the revision of Article XIII in 1965 a case such as that involving Acierto was within the jurisdiction of United States courts-martial under both the agreement and United States law.[73] In spite of this expansion of jurisdiction, however, it appears that Acierto in 1948 was the last Filipino, either employed or otherwise, who was tried by United States courts-martial.[74] The reason for the failure of the United States to exercise jurisdiction after this date is not known. Perhaps the United States felt that not exercising jurisdiction would help to maintain good diplomatic relations with the Philippines and/or to further the establishment of good relations between the bases and the local communites.

Olongapo. Of related interest to the court-martial of Filipino nationals was the situation which existed at Olongapo from the end of World War II to December 1959. Olongapo, as has been noted earlier, was a barrio within the municipality of Subic and at the same time within the Subic Bay naval reservation.[75] As early as November 1946 difficulties over conflicts of jurisdiction developed. At that time it was reported that

> charges of abusive treatment and unwarranted beatings of Filipinos by Marines and taxation of Filipino concessonaires and townfolk were the result of an alleged investigation by one reporter on the naval reservation... [who] interviewed 11 Filipinos who recited a long list of real or imagined abuses.[76]

[72] Article 2, paragraph 12, Uniform Code of Military Justice, 64 *Stat.* 107 (1950). See also *Operation Hearings 1955*, p. 37.

[73] In a series of cases from 1957 to 1960, the United States Supreme Court ruled that courts-martial do not have jurisdiction over civilians who are protected by the provisions of the United States Constitution. For the cases involved, see below, chap. VI, note 7. Since the provisions of Article 2, paragraph 12, of the Uniform Code of Military Justice were not challenged before United States courts, it is not clear how the Supreme Court of the United States would have ruled on the provisions of that paragraph which allowed the trial of Filipinos by United States courts-martial under the provisions of the 1947 agreement. The question becomes moot under the 1965 agreement because such trials are prohibited.

[74] Research undertaken in the Philippines for the author indicates that in about 1947 or 1948 there was one other case in which a Filipino national was tried by a court-martial. This trial occurred at Subic Bay, but trial records are not available. The source of this information is confidential.

[75] See above, pp. 7–9.

[76] *New York Times*, November 9, 1946, p. 9. This report was made in the *Philippine Liberty*

Because of such reports President Roxas requested Representative Magsaysay to conduct an official investigation. According to Magsaysay's findings manhandling by Marines had occurred at Olongapo, but "these were isolated cases, not following any set pattern." He stressed the readiness of the United States personnel to correct abuses when the facts were brought to the attention of the Commandant.[77]

Apparently in the next several years the situation at Olongapo produced few problems which received publicity. There is evidence that in 1948 a verbal order was issued by the Commander, United States Naval Forces in the Philippines, directing that the administration of justice within Olongapo by the naval authorities be discontinued.[78] This order may have reduced friction temporarily.

Not until 1955 did press reports again make a major issue of the situation at Olongapo. Meyer noted that in July of that year the *Manila Chronicle*

> featured articles on alleged treatment of Filipinos..., in the Olongapo area, as second class citizens in their own country. The articles reported that Filipinos on the base complained of summary deportation from the reservation without due process of law, arbitrary American military intervention in civilian functions properly belonging to the municipal government of Subic..., discrimination against Filipinos in favor of aliens in granting business concessions, and excessive taxation.[79]

Such reports once again led to a Philippine government investigation. Under Secretary of Foreign Affairs Neri, who was in charge of the investigation, reported that conditions at Olongapo "could stand a lot of improvement," and that the base authorities had agreed to make changes. As Meyer stated:

> In time, the Navy turned over the administration of the base high schools to the Philippine Government, relaxed the enforcement of car registration at checkpoints, revised the system of fees, made the membership of the town council entirely elec-

News, November 8, 1946, and went so far as to say that the marine detail at the base was "as bad as the Japs." As cited in *New York Times*, November 10, 1946, p. 51. As a result of the report the United States Navy allowed United States and Filipino newsmen on the base with free movement. It was reported by the *New York Times* that "no complainants could be found saying the Americans were 'as bad as the Japs.'" Nevertheless, there were reports of maltreatment by the marines and twenty-five Filipino prisoners were reported to be in the reservation jail. *Ibid.*

[77] See *ibid.*, November 18, 1946, p. 10. A naval investigation undertaken at the same time indicated that a few isolated "anomalies" had been discovered and corrective steps taken. *Ibid.*, November 9, 1946, p. 9.

[78] The source of this information is confidential.

[79] Meyer, pp. 289–290, citing the *Sunday Chronicle*, July 3, 1955, pp. 1, 12; the *Manila Chronicle*, July 4, 1955, pp. 1, 9; *ibid.*, July 5, 1955, pp. 1, 12; *ibid.*, July 6, 1955, pp. 1, 12; *ibid.*, July 7, 1955, pp. 1, 7. See also *New York Times*, July 12, 1955, p. 8; and *ibid.*, August 21, 1955, p. 12.

tive,[80] and facilitated the entry of Philippine Government officials into the... reservation to enable them to perform their duties.[81]

Although these changes improved conditions, the friction in Olongapo did not cease. In July 1959 a report in *Time* called attention to numerous alleged abuses toward Filipinos by the naval authorities, including search without warrant, detention for not having the proper identification, and administrative "deportation" of "undesirables" from the barrio.[82]

Due to such circumstances the Filipinos continued to press for the return of Olongapo to the Philippines, and finally in December 1959 the area was turned over by the United States.[83] The right of the United States to exercise jurisdiction over Filipinos for on-base offenses, however, was not taken away at that time. As has been noted, the United States apparently did not exercise such jurisdiction after 1948, and at no time did it exercise jurisdiction over a Filipino who was not an employee of the United States. The fact that the United States retained this right, however, was objected to strongly by the Filipinos.[84]

Killing and Injury of Filipinos by Security Guards on the Bases

Another important problem in Philippine-United States relations, and certainly the major problem in later years insofar as the jurisdictional question was concerned, arose out of the killing and wounding of Filipinos on the bases by security guards of the United States. In some cases these guards were members of the United States military force; in others they were Filipino employees of security agencies under contract to the United States military. The United States, under the provisions of Article XIII, paragraph 1(a), had the right to exercise jurisdiction over guards who were members of the United States armed

[80] Present author's note. It was later reported that six of the nine Filipino members of this "showcase" city council worked for the Navy and had not shown "much inclination to vote against their employer." In case they decided to do so, the navy commander in charge of Olongapo had "the power to veto." *Time*, July 20, 1959, p. 34.

[81] Meyer, p. 290, citing 51 *Off. Gaz.* cccxxxii (1955). It was reported in December 1959 that Rear Admiral Spring, the Commanding Officer at Subic Bay, had announced the ouster of Commander West, the administrator of Olongapo, "for rudeness" to Philippine authorities. Reportedly, West "had said he did not 'give a damn' when asked to help in the service of Philippine court orders," and Admiral Spring had stated that "he would 'not tolerate such behavior among my staff officers.'" See Locsin, *Free Press*, December 5, 1959, p. 59.

[82] *Time*, July 20, 1959, p. 34. See also Locsin, *Free Press*, July 25, 1959, pp. 3–4.

[83] See below, chapter V, note 92.

[84] See, in particular, de Castro, pp. 643–647.

forces. According to paragraphs 1(a) and 2, however, offenses committed by Filipino guards against fellow Filipinos apparently were subject to Philippine jurisdiction.[85]

The central legal question in offenses involving killings and injuries by security guards arose out of the fact that, generally speaking, under Philippine law an offended person in a criminal offense is allowed to respond only to the extent necessary to repel the aggressor. Thus, in minor robbery or trespassing cases, which most of the cases on the bases were, the offended cannot legally shoot the criminal unless there is "reasonable cause."[86] More important than the legal interpretation of "reasonable cause," however, was the question of the killing or the injuring of Filipinos by Americans or their employees. The matter, therefore, became involved with the whole question of Philippine sovereignty and national dignity.

The killing of Filipinos on the bases was one aspect of the United States operations in the Philippines that was kept out of the public eye as much as possible. In recent years, however, several "headline" cases arose which could not be covered up. Through these cases information was disclosed which previously was unavailable.

In order to understand the United States point of view it is necessary to consider the security problem which exists on some of the United States bases. According to a December 1964 report of the United States Embassy in the Philippines, this problem was particularly serious at Clark Field,[87] where in 1964 alone 564 bombs were stolen, some of which weighed as much as 500 pounds. The theft of running lights also was a serious problem—six were stolen in September and thirteen in the first two and a half weeks of December.[88] On one occasion it was reported in the Philippine press that Governor Aquino of Tarlac Province had related how a radar tower at Clark Field had "collapsed when looters pulled off its cables." The reporter noted: "For Clark, this meant 20 frantic minutes of a blackout in communications: what

[85] See above, chap. III, note 12; and below, pp. 73–74.

[86] Interview with provincial Governor Jose Sering in New Orleans, May 29, 1966. See also Rama, *Free Press*, December 26, 1964, p. 2.

[87] Few problems have arisen at Sangley Point except for petty pilferage. The situation is more serious at Subic Bay but not as serious as at Clark Field. It has been noted that a yearly average of 125 "intruders" are apprehended at Clark Field and turned over to the local authorities in Tarlac Province and Pampanga Province. Rama, *Free Press*, December 26, 1964, p. 2. As of April 14, 1966, there was a total of 256 Philippine nationals being prosecuted in the Philippine courts for offenses committed on Clark Field. Personal letter from Captain Hackett, dated April 14, 1966.

[88] See *New York Times*, December 19, 1964, p. 7. See also *ibid.*, August 11, 1959, p. 29; *ibid.*, December 28, 1964, p. 13; and *ibid.*, August 1, 1966, p. 26.

if war had broken out at that time? But for the looters, it merely meant 20 pesos' worth of wire."[89]

According to one source there was an organized group of "gangsters" that operated around Clark Air Base. These gangsters, it was reported, worked on a percentage basis for powerful Chinese and Philippine businessmen in the local area. The bombs were stolen in order to extract the powder for sale to fishermen, while the casings were sold for scrap metal. The success and continuation of such activities may have been the result of cooperation between "businessmen" and local politicians.[90] Although these reports were made recently, the security problem was an old one, dating back to the reoccupation of the Philippines by the United States forces toward the end of World War II.[91]

In addition to such illegal activities another basic problem on the bases has been the apparently legal but nevertheless dangerous activity of simply gathering scrap metal. De Manila, a Philippine newspaperman, gave some insight into this problem when he reported the events of a court-martial at Clark Field. De Manila stated:

> The [military] court had laughed when told that Filipinos at Crow Valley "catch bombs." How could a people who were not scared of falling bombs be scared away by a warning rifle shot? The bombs are duds, dropped during target practice by planes... On the peripheries of the bull's-eye wait the Filipinos, and as soon as a bomb has dropped they race each other to the site to plant their stake. Who gets his stake in first gets the bomb afterwards—but he has to get out of there fast because there's only a few minutes interval between one bomb and the next... Yet the "bomb-catchers" of Crow Valley are nothing compared to the "bomb-catchers" in another part of Clark, the part where they explode defective or damaged bombs. When it's bomb exploding time there, the Filipinos hover around the site—"like vultures," says a Filipino army officer—and race each other to snatch at the still-smoking bombs. Many of them have lost fingers or hands or eyes in this occupation, but are still there, hovering and quarreling like vultures, when bombs are exploded.[92]

In addition to the type of activity which de Manila reported, there was a great deal of less spectacular scavenging in which Filipinos merely search for scrap metal or other types of discarded goods.

From such a situation involving both illegal and legal activity arose the two main purposes of the security guards on the bases—first, to protect United States property and personnel, and, second, to protect Filipinos from putting themselves in danger. At Clark Field these security guards were both military personnel and Filipino civilian employees under contract through the Negrito Guard Agency. Most of

[89] Quijano de Manila, *Free Press*, March 6, 1965, p. 67.
[90] The source of this information is confidential.
[91] See *New York Times*, July 24, 1959, p. 6.
[92] De Manila, *Free Press*, March 6, 1965, p. 70.

the deaths at Clark Field were at the hands of the civilian employees. It was reported in 1959 that some twenty suspected Filipino pilferers had "been shot and killed by Filipino security guards at Clark... in the past 10 years or so." The situation was complicated by the fact that these guards were members of indigenous tribes, pagans in an overwhelmingly Catholic country and in some ways "wards" of the United States military. In many cases they hated and resented the Christian population of the Philippines and often were more loyal to the United States than they were to the Philippines. It was reported that they had been abused by the Philippine government and politicians and looked to American personnel for protection. United States personnel responded by giving clothes, food, and other items to the tribesmen.

Since the civilian guards at Clark Field were drawn from this population, the question arose as to the treatment they would receive if prosecuted by the Philippine authorities for offenses committed while on duty protecting United States personnel and property. If the United States had turned over an accused Filipino guard to the Philippine authorities they would have run the risk of losing the loyality of these guards which was virtually complete.[93] This situation represented one important aspect of the jurisdictional problem, at least at Clark Air Base.[94]

Much of the Philippine dissatisfaction with the existing situation was brought out in a 1959 newspaper report by Tutay.[95] He noted that there had been no Philippine investigation of killings at Clark Field because the United States authorities had claimed "exclusive jurisdiction" in such cases under the agreement of 1947. As Tutay pointed out, this position was and had been untenable.[96] Only when such an offense was committed by United States personnel did the United States have jurisdiction. On the other hand, offenses by Filipino civilian guards against fellow Filipinos came under Philippine jurisdiction.[97] The latter point received emphasis when the Philippine Supreme Court specifically stated in the *Miquiabas* case that as a civilian employee of

[93] The source of this information is confidential.

[94] Apparently no such problem exists at Sangley Point. The Legal Officer there stated: "The civilian guards are hired in the local community, and generally follow the local ethnic patterns... Insofar as fairness of treatment is concerned, I have seen little to indicate [that] there would be any particular bias against these men in the local courts." Personal letter from Commander Davis, dated May 26, 1966.

[95] Filemon V. Tutay, *Free Press*, May 16, 1959, p. 6. At the invitation of Lt. Colonel Edward Kandel, Information Service Chief, Tutay had gone to Clark Field to look into the killings on the base.

[96] *Ibid.*

[97] See above, Chap. III, note 12.

the United States, Miquiabas was not to be considered a member of the United States military forces.[98] Certainly the civilian guards on the bases could not have been classified as anything other than civilian employees of the United States. In fact, as has been pointed out, at Clark Field the guards were not directly but rather indirectly employed by the United States Air Force.[99]

In spite of the legality of Philippine jurisdiction in cases involving Philippine guards, the local authorities, as Tutay noted, did not dispute the United States military authorities' claim of exclusive jurisdiction. On being questioned by Tutay, a "high security officer," who refused to be identified, stated that the general procedure followed when a suspected thief was killed by a guard was:

(1) place the security guard involved under technical arrest; (2) send for a priest or ambulance; (3) call the [United States Air Force] OSI (Office of Special Investigation) and the Philippine Constabulary [PC] detachment at Angeles, Pampanga, which is the nearest PC unit from the air base; and (4) then turn over the body of the victim (in case of death) to his family.[100]

Tutay also asked this security officer "why nothing has been done about the killings since the beginning like the routine filing of an information [criminal complaint] with the proper court." The reply was that "this is probably due to the belief of the PC [Philippine Constabulary] that they were justified homicide." In checking this out, Tutay questioned the local PC unit and was told that "the PC had been only 'notified' by the air base authorities of the cases of killings in Clark Field and that the PC command in Pampanga had 'never made any investigation of these cases because of the American claim of exclusive jurisdiction.'"[101]

Tutay reported that eventually Provincial Fiscal Kayanan attempted to conduct an investigation into the deaths. He took statements from witnesses and found that allegedly some of the bodies had had as many as fifteen gunshot wounds. Kayanan also requested that the Air Force supply him with copies of their investigation reports. These were supplied "but only after the signatures, the names of the security guards involved and even the initials which authenticated some corrections had been meticulously deleted from the reports." After completing this part of this investigation Fiscal Kayanan stated:

[98] *Miquiabas* v. *Commanding General*, 80 Phil. 262, 268–269 (1948).

[99] See Salvador L. Mariño (Secretary of Justice), *Report to President Macapagal on the U.S. Bases Incidents* [dated January 30, 1965] (Manila: Ilagan and Sanga Press, n.d.) [hereafter *Mariño Report*], p. 22. This report may also be found in 3 *PILJ* 535, 535–550 (1964).

[100] Tutay, *Free Press*, May 16, 1959, p. 6.

[101] *Ibid.*, pp. 6–7.

There is a clear admission that all the victims were killed by Filipino Security guards of Clark AB (Air Base). The *modus operandi* in all cases was practically uniform, in that the victims were running away after ignoring the challenge to halt when they were shot and killed. The security guards are under instruction to apprehend and identify any person sighted in the area and to prevent the removal of U.S. property from the base, and in so preventing they are required to fire three (3) warning shots into the air, but if the oral challenge and the warning shots have no effect, the guards are to take such action as might be necessary to prevent their escape, to include firing upon them, as a last resort.[102]

On the basis of his evidence Kayanan "believed that 'the *prima facie* crimes of murder have been committed, and that all the security guards involved in the killings are probably guilty thereof.'" To proceed with his cases, however, Kayanan needed the names of the guards, which the Air Force authorities refused to release. In an attempt to get these names Kayanan took the problem to Secretary of Justice Barrera, but Barrera was no more successful than Kayanan had been. Eventually the problem was referred to Secretary of Foreign Affairs Serrano, who in turn contacted the United States Embassy in Manila. Tutay stated that talks were prolonged over several months because the United States government took the position "that it could not be indifferent to the fate of its employees for the consequence of their acts while engaged in the proper performance of their duties." Finally, however, the United States gave up its claim of "exclusive jurisdiction," and "in due time" the names of ten guards were released by the United States military authorities. Nevertheless, stated Tutay, Kayanan was unable to prosecute because he lacked some documents that the United States authorities "consistently refused to release."[103] Perhaps, as de Castro suggested, the military authorities' refusal to cooperate was due to their concern with retaining good morale among the Filipino guards.[104]

Tutay noted that after the last killing in 1958 the base commander at Clark Air Base issued orders that security guards were "to be armed only with shotguns loaded with bird shot in order to minimize the possibility of killing alleged pilferers." This was introduced, the commander stated, "in the interest of Philippine-American relations." Fiscal Kayanan, "in acknowledging the base commander's generous gesture," Tutay stated, "assured him that every effort would be exerted

[102] *Ibid.*, p. 7. The guards were instructed to "fire low" if a thief did not stop after a third warning. See *New York Times*, July 24, 1959, p. 6.
[103] Tutay, *Free Press*, May 16, 1959, p. 7.
[104] De Castro, pp. 642–643.

to discourage thievery at Clark Field by promptly prosecuting all intruders apprehended at the base."[105]

The publication of Tutay's article in May 1959 apparently had little effect on subsequent prosecution of Filipino guards. Secretary of Justice Mariño reported in January 1965 that only a small percentage of the cases involving the killing of Filipinos was investigated by the provincial fiscals concerned. Most of the cases "did not receive official attention and indeed passed with scant public notice..."[106]

According to Mariño's report, of the "list of cases in the Department of Justice, only seven are said to involve American servicemen guards..."[107] In each of these cases involving United States servicemen

> the cases were closed... upon investigation by base authorities which led to the determination that there was no criminal responsibility and [the men] were allowed to leave the Philippines upon termination of their tours of duty.[108]

Two additional cases which occurred in 1964 attracted considerable attention and prompted President Macapagal to direct Secretary of Justice Mariño to conduct an immediate investigation. One of these cases, the Cole case, involved the killing of Rogilio Balagtas at Clark Field and the other, the Edwards-Thomas case, involved the killing of Gonzalo Villedo at Subic Bay Naval Base. In both cases the United States personnel were tried by court-martial. Because of their publicity and consequent influence on Philippine-United States relations these two cases will be discussed in detail.

On November 25, 1964, Airman 1st-Class Larry Dean Cole was on guard duty at Clark Air Base from 5:00 A.M. until 3:30 P.M. Cole's duty, among other things, "was to guard the restricted area from trespassers primarily to protect their lives during target practice." Crow Valley, the restricted area in question, was a gunnery range used by the Philippine Air Force and the United States Air Force for target practice. Scrap metal was present in the area and in spite of the fact that it was a restricted area "civilians gathered scrap iron or empty ammunition shells as a source of income."[109]

At about 5:00 P.M. on the same day Cole went out to hunt birds with a privately owned .22 caliber rifle. At approximately 5:30 he saw several people in the restricted area. He fired a warning shot in the air

[105] Tutay, *Free Press*, May 16, 1959, p. 74.
[106] *Mariño Report*, p. 12.
[107] *Ibid.* Mariño's complete list included twenty-eight cases with the first occurring in April 1947 and the last in August 1963. This list did not include the Balagtas and Villedo deaths of November and December 1964. For the lists of victims, see *ibid.*, p. 11.
[108] *Ibid.*, p. 12.
[109] *Ibid.*, p. 2.

and the trespassers fled through the brush toward a nearby river. Cole fired three more shots and then allegedly resumed his hunting, returning to the barracks some twenty minutes later. The body of Rogelio Balagtas y Manzano "(half-breed Baluga or Negrito), 16, single, Filipino, resident of Barrio Crow Valley, Capas, Tarlac" was found near the riverbank in a small cave at about 7:00 P.M. that evening.[110]

Balagtas was a member of the Baluga tribe of pygmy-like Negrito people living in the Crow Valley area of Clark Air Base. Beginning in 1957 the United States Air Force officials at Clark had started tolerating the influx of Baluga tribesmen into this area. Reportedly "some 5,000 families had entered the area, setting up huts and cultivating vegetable patches."[111] Rogelio Balagtas lived in one of the huts built near the target range.

The morning after Balagtas' body was found an autopsy was performed, and it was determined that he had died of shock after having been hit in the head with a bullet. The slug was submitted to the United States Army, and it was confirmed that the bullet had been fired from a gun used by Cole.[112]

Six days later the father of the victim received 3,150 pesos ($787) from the United States government "'in full satisfaction of damages arising as a consequence of the death of his son.' He executed a 'Release of Claim and Affidavit of Desistance'."[113] Subsequently the Air Force filed charges of unpremeditated murder against Cole.[114]

Insofar as United States public relations in the Philippines were concerned, it was extremely important that it was not until forty-five days after the event that the Philippine newspapers discovered that Airman Cole had been off duty and on a personal hunting expedition when the killing of Balagtas took place.[115] According to Trumbull, "the local police were given all the facts, but apparently nothing was done by the military to inform the local press that anything had occurred." The result of this handling of the killing was that the Philippine press seemed "to be under the impression that the American military had

[110] *Ibid.*, pp. 2–3.

[111] *Free Press*, January 16, 1965, p. 66. See also Robert Trumbull, *New York Times*, January 15, 1965, p. 3.

[112] *Mariño Report*, pp. 3–4.

[113] See *ibid.*, p. 4; and *New York Times*, December 5, 1964, p. 25.

[114] See *New York Times*, December 9, 1964, p. 7; and *ibid.*, December 25, 1964, p. 10.

[115] Trumbull, *New York Times*, January 15, 1965, p. 3. While Secretary Mariño was conducting his on-the-spot inquiry into the facts surrounding the incident at Clark Field, he was told by Cole's immediate superior that Cole was on duty in that he "was on duty 24 hours a day on the range [with the task of clearing off 'intruders'], but his 'official duty day' ceased at 3:30 P.M." *Free Press*, January 16, 1965, p. 66.

hoped the incident would escape public notice." Consequently when the press discovered that Cole was off duty, they gave the story "banner headlines" in the Sunday papers. Trumbull reported that the press created an image "of 'bloodthirsty' and 'trigger-happy' young sentries 'wantonly killing Filipinos.'"[116] In this atmosphere the press and the public "clamored" for Philippine jurisdiction over Cole and the two marines involved in the killing of Villedo at Subic Bay Naval Base.[117] At least two rallies were held in Manila, at which time "Uncle Sam" was burned in effigy, Yankee-go-home placards were displayed, and thirty-one coffins representing the Filipinos killed by security guards on the bases were exhibited.[118]

With respect to the Cole case Secretary Mariño's January 1965 report concluded that there was

> prima facie evidence that would warrant the filing of an information for homicide [the equivalent of the unpremeditated murder charge earlier set forth by the air force] as penalized under Article 249 [of the Philippine Revised Penal Code].

The payment of civil indemnity, he noted, did not extinguish or bar criminal prosecution. However, Mariño further stated that the provisions of the 1947 agreement had to be considered. Since the crime had been committed about six miles within the military reservation, he stated, the United States had jurisdiction.[119]

On February 23, 1965, Cole's court-martial began.[120] Cole pleaded not guilty to the charge of unpremeditated murder for which the maximum penalty was life imprisonment.[121] Apparently the only fact in dispute was whether or not Cole had aimed his rifle before firing. Cole maintained that he had fired a warning shot in the general

[116] Trumbull, *New York Times*, January 15, 1965, p. 3.

[117] See *Free Press*, August 21, 1965, p. 90.

[118] See *ibid.*; and *ibid.*, January 30, 1965, p. 66. Press denunciations of the killings at Clark Field and Subic Bay eventually led to a conference between United States Ambassador William McCormick Blair, Jr. and President Diosdado Macapagal. *New York Times*, December 23, 1964, p. 17. No results of this conference have been published. It may be significant, however, that one day before the conference Foreign Secretary Mauro Mendez announced that the Philippines "would ask" the United States to waive jurisdiction over the two cases. *Ibid.*, December 22, 1964, p. 17. Two days after the conference Mendez announced that the Philippines "may ask" for jurisdiction. *Ibid.*, December 25, 1964, p. 10. Apparently the Philippines never did ask for jurisdiction. See Trumbull, *ibid.*, December 25, 1964, p. 10; Oscar S. Villadolid, *Manila Daily Bulletin*, February 3, 1965; Ernesto del Rosario, *Manila Chronicle*, February 1, 1965; and the [Philippine] *Examiner*, February 14, 1965. It may be that an American concession as to the jurisdictional question was obtained during the meeting between Blair and Macapagal, with the formally declared agreement coming eight months later.

[119] *Mariño Report*, p. 5.

[120] For details of the trial proceedings, see de Manila, *Free Press*, March 6, 1965, pp. 3, 67–71.

[121] See *New York Times*, February 24, 1965, p. 10.

direction of a group of trespassers. He stated that he did not fire with the intention of killing or wounding any of the youths and that he did not see any of the boys fall. He had no indication, he stated, that anyone had been hit. In opposition to Cole's testimony, two Filipino witnesses stated that Cole had aimed his rifle at the trespassers before he fired.[122]

The court-martial found Cole guilty as charged and sentenced him to three years confinement with hard labor, demoted him to private, and gave him a dishonorable discharge.[123] Apparently the Filipinos were satisfied with both the trial proceedings and the sentence handed down by the court-martial. Some of this satisfaction was due to the fact that the trial was attended by Chief State Prosecutor Gancayco, an official representative of the Philippine government, Senator Fernandez, and Governor Aquino of Tarlac Province.[124] After the trial Gancayco stated:

> The members of the court-martial demonstrated complete impartiality in passing judgment. The penalty imposed is reasonable, and falls within the range of Philippine penalities for homicide, which is the equivalent of the charge against Cole.[125]

In connection with the sentence imposed, de Manila noted that after the verdict of guilty had been handed down it was not expected that Cole would get the maximum sentence, and "the Filipinos [were] content that [Cole] had been found guilty as charged, [and] now prayed unanimously for a lenient sentence."[126]

By no means was everyone as satisfied with the court-martial decision as was the Philippine public. An important aspect of the Cole case which should not be overlooked was pointed out by Cole's attorney in his summation. He stated that "over a period of years, many outsiders and many intruders have been fired upon and shot." Yet no prior trial of this nature had been held. He then asked "why" Cole was now on trial, and answered the question by stating that Cole was a "hopeless pawn in an episode of international negotiations and intrigue."[127] It does appear that, in some respects at least, Cole was a victim of Philippine-United States foreign relations. The very fact that he was tried seemed to suggest this. That Philippine observers were present at the trial further indicated the precariousness of his position.

[122] See *ibid.*, February 26, 1965, p. 2. See also *Mariño Report*, p. 4.

[123] See *New York Times*, February 26, 1965, p. 2; *ibid.*, February 27, 1965, p. 7; and de Manila, *Free Press*, March 6, 1965, p. 71.

[124] *Ibid.*, p. 67.

[125] As quoted in *ibid.*, p. 71.

[126] *Ibid.*

[127] As quoted in *ibid.*, p. 70. See also *New York Times*, February 26, 1965, p. 2.

De Manila noted that the presence of official Philippine government observers was, in fact, a departure from the previous policy of United States military authorities in court-martial proceedings in the Philippines.[128] Apparently, it was highly important to the Philippine government that the United States had been concerned enough about Philippine reaction to the Cole case to invite official observers to the trial. An additional non-legal aspect of the criminal jurisdiction question can be seen in the reaction of Senator Manahan when he learned that Cole's sentence had been altered to include a bad conduct rather than a dishonorable discharge.[129] This action was denounced promptly by Manahan and three other Philippine senators. Manahan was reported to have said that this showed that "Americans are taking us for granted."[130] This fear of being "taken for granted" was probably one of the things Trumbull was referring to when he stated:

> The passions bared after the two recent incidents [the deaths of Balagtas and Villedo] have deeper roots than any solicitude for the obscure victims of the tragedies. There has been a total lack of indignation over the slaying of at least six Filipino guards on the bases by armed thieves of their own nationality in recent years.[131]

With respect to Philippine-United States relations the ideas of being "taken for granted," of "lack of trust" by the United States, and of such things as "national pride" and "national sovereignty" are found repeatedly in the writings of Filipinos. In a recent conversation with Jose Sering, a Philippine provincial governor, the author noted the constant reference to the "national pride" of the Filipinos and the "lack of trust" in the Philippines by the United States.[132]

The international relations aspect of the Cole trial appears to be confirmed at least partially by the Philippine reaction to the court-martial of Corporal Jesse Allen Edwards and Lance Corporal James Bradford Thomas for the killing of Gonzalo Villedo.[133] Edwards and Thomas were on "stakeout duty" at Subic Bay Naval Base near a restricted area where a naval ammunition magazine was located. Their task was to apprehend or drive out intruders from the area.[134] According to the report of Secretary Mariño, the official version of the Subic Bay authorities was that at about 7:00 P.M. on December 13, 1964, a boat with a

[128] De Manila, *Free Press*, March 6, 1965, p. 67.
[129] The reviewing authority, Major General Sam Maddox Jr., the 13th Air Force Commander, had so altered Cole's sentence. *New York Times*, April 22, 1965, p. 11.
[130] As quoted in *ibid.*
[131] Trumbull, *New York Times*, January 31, 1965, IV, p. 10.
[132] Interview with Governor Sering in New Orleans, May 29, 1966.
[133] For details of the trial proceedings, see de Manila, *Free Press*, March 13, 1965, pp. 3, 81.
[134] Felipe Lagon, *Free Press*, January 23, 1965, p. 64.

light came near shore where Edwards and Thomas were located. The men in the boat were challenged by the marines but no response was received. When the boat was approximately fifteen feet from the shoreline the marines fired warning shots in the water and in the air. Two men, one holding a lamp, went into the water and then the boat drifted out from the shore, either pushed or pulled by someone in the water. The marines left the post and reported the events. Allegedly they did not know anyone was hurt.[135]

The version of Ricardo Villedo, one of the occupants of the boat and brother of the victim, was substantially different from that of the marines. He stated that he and his brother, Gonzalo, were about 100 meters from the shore when they were yelled at and immediately fired upon. Gonzalo Villedo fell into the water with the first shot, and after hearing four more shots Ricardo stated that he jumped into the water and pulled the boat toward the sea. When Gonzalo did not appear, Ricardo left and later found blood in the boat. Later that night the body of Gonzalo Villedo was recovered about 75 meters from the shore. An autopsy by a Philippine official found that the body had a wound in the right ear. No whole slug but rather only fragments were found, indicating that the slug probably had shattered on impact with the water.[136]

The "findings" of the Secretary of Justice in his investigation were that the place where the body was found "corroborated" the story of Ricardo Villedo that he and his brother were 100 meters from the shore. Gonzalo Villedo, Mariño stated, "no doubt" was killed by one of the two marines and the evidence indicated that the marines did not use "due caution" when firing "what they called 'warning shots'." He further noted, however, that the offense evidently was committed inside the naval base and hence the United States had jurisdiction.[137]

The United States announced on February 9 that Thomas and Edwards would be tried for negligent homicide in the death of Villedo.[138] On March 9, it was stated that the court-martial had found Thomas and Edwards not guilty. The finding of the court-martial was that both were on duty at the time of the incident and had opened fire only when the fishermen disregarded warnings to halt.[139]

As in the Cole case the Philippines had an official representative, Chief Legal Counsel Buenaventura de la Fuente of the Justice Depart-

135 *Mariño Report*, pp. 7–8.

136 *Ibid.*, pp. 8–9.

137 *Ibid.*, pp. 9–10.

138 *New York Times*, February 10, 1965, p. 8.

139 *Ibid.*, March 9, 1965, p. 11.

ment, at the court-martial.[140] The Thomas-Edwards trial, however, seemed to be far less important to the Filipinos than the Cole trial had been. As de Manila noted, the trial at Subic Bay was "anticlimatic after the drama of the judgment at Clark [Air Base]."[141] The trial itself was more dull, fewer newsmen from Manila came, and, in general, there seemed to be less interest in this case after Cole had been pronounced guilty.[142] Apparently the results of the Cole trial—and specifically the fact that an American had been tried for killing a Filipino by the United States itself—had at least for the time being partially satisfied the national pride of the Filipinos. The issue was not closed, however, and the Philippine foreign office continued to press for a new criminal jurisdictional arrangement. Apparently the Philippine government was becoming tired of the usual procedure. As Locsin, the editor of the *Philippines Free Press* said in January 1965:

> We have had enough of double talk. That's why there has been no agreement on jurisdiction after so many years of negotiations. That's why the killings have gone on with no justice done. There would be negotiations, then suspension of negotiations, then more killings, then resumption of negotiations, that is, more double talk, leading to more killings and still no justice done, encouraging the killing of more Filipinos by American servicemen.[143]

Locsin may have overstated the point, but it does appear that in early 1965 the Philippine government became extremely eager to obtain a revision of the 1947 agreement.

Summary

The problem areas discussed in this chapter include problems produced by conflicts of jurisdiction and jurisdictional lacunae. Many of these problems arose out of the jurisdictional arrangements established by the Military Bases Agreement. Other problems resulted from administrative practices and connections between politics and crime. Although such problems exist in some degree everywhere, the situation in the Philippines seemed to influence substantially the operation of the jurisdictional arrangements of the 1947 agreement.

[140] De Manila, *Free Press*, March 13, 1965, p. 81.
[141] *Ibid.*
[142] See *ibid.*
[143] Locsin, *Free Press*, January 9, 1965, p. 8.

CHAPTER V

REVISION OF THE 1947 AGREEMENT

During the early years of Philippine independence the question of the criminal jurisdictional arrangements of the 1947 agreement attracted little attention. The attempts to revise these arrangements had their beginning in July 1953 and continued periodically through August 1965. Within this twelve year period, four phases of negotiation are distinguishable, each of which will be discussed in this chapter. In the background of the revision attempts were the general problems of Philippine security and sovereignty. These problems will be discussed briefly.

The Security-Sovereignty Dilemma

Of utmost importance to the Philippines from the granting of independence to the outbreak of the Korean War was the lack of a "formal guarantee" stating that in case of attack by outside aggressors the United States would come immediately to its aid. No such formal guarantee had been included in the 1947 agreement. The United States merely had given verbal assurance to the Filipinos that "any attack on them would be considered dangerous to American peace and safety."[1] It was the failure to obtain a more definite commitment from the United States that led Liberal Congressman Atienza in March 1949 to demand a re-examination of United States-Philippine treaties. Apparently he had some doubt as to whether the United States would defend the Philippines if war were to occur with Russia.[2] Two years later in early 1951, in the face of United Nations reversals in Korea and the increased attention of United States policy toward Europe and away from Asia, General Romulo stated that some Filipinos were beginning to wonder whether "we should re-examine our foreign policy, particularly that aspect of it which calls for close cooperation with the United States of America."[3]

[1] Taylor, p. 129.
[2] *New York Times*, March 4, 1949, p. 15; and *ibid.*, March 15, 1949, p. 4.
[3] *Ibid.*, January 7, 1951, p. 12.

Although neither of these statements was aimed at breaking with the United States, the United States felt called upon to give firmer assurance of its intention to protect the Philippines. Initially this assurance was set forth verbally, first by Ambassador Cowen[4] and later by President Truman. The President announced that "the whole world knows that the United States recognizes that an armed attack on the Philippines would be looked upon by the United States as dangerous to its own safety and that it would act accordingly."[5] The Filipinos were not satisfied completely with this verbal commitment. Senator Recto, among others, wanted something more than a United States obligation to "act accordingly."[6] In June he condemned United States policy as "vacillating" and reportedly demanded that "the Philippines require ironclad guarantees for its defense or adopt strict neutrality."[7]

The extent of the influence of such intense Philippine criticism on United States action is not known, but in August 1951 the Mutual Defense Treaty between the two states was announced.[8] The preamble to the treaty states that one of its primary purposes is

> to declare publicly and formally their sense of unity and common determination to defend themselves against external armed attack, so that no potential aggressor could be under the illusion that either of them stands alone in the Pacific area...

Article IV of the treaty further states:

> Each party recognizes that an armed attack in the Pacific area on either of the Parties would be dangerous to its own peace and safety and declares that it would act to meet the common dangers in accordance with its constitutional process.

In May 1952 the Mutual Defense Treaty was ratified by both governments. Ratification was unanimously recommended by the Philippine Senate and consented to by a voice vote in the United States Senate.[9] Even before ratification President Quirino stressed that the treaty as-

[4] See *ibid.*, January 20, 1951, p. 3.

[5] Statement by President Truman, released to the press on April 18, 1951, 24 *Department of State Bulletin* 699, 699 (1951). See also a similar statement by Secretary of State Acheson, *New York Times*, July 26, 1951, p. 1.

[6] *Free Press*, April 28, 1951, pp. 2–3. See also *Manila Times*, July 26, 1951, p. 1.

[7] *New York Times*, June 16, 1951, p. 32.

[8] Mutual Defense Treaty. Signed at Washington August 30, 1951; entered into force August 27, 1952. 3 *UST* 3947; *TIAS* 2529.

[9] See *New York Times*, March 2, 1952, p. 1; *ibid.*, April 16, 1952, p. 1; *ibid.*, May 13, 1952, p. 2; 98 *Congressional Record* 2594 (1952). When the United States Senate consented to ratification on March 20, 1952, no discussion of the treaty took place. Eleven days later, on motions to reconsider the United States-Philippine treaty and the security treaty between Australia, New Zealand, and the United States (which also had been consented to on March 20), Senator Watkins briefly discussed the Philippine treaty. He withdrew his motion, however, and no further discussion of the treaty occurred in the United States Congress. See *ibid.*, pp. 3227–3232.

sured Philippine security from external aggression.[10] Additional steps were taken in this direction in October 1952, when the United States agreed to strengthen its bases in the Philippines and further aid the Philippine military,[11] and in September 1954, when the Southeast Asia Collective Defense Treaty was signed. Article IV of the Southeast Asia treaty is virtually the same as Article IV of the Mutual Defense Treaty with the exception of the extension of the provisions to include six countries in addition to the United States and the Philippines.[12] These developments seemed to set the security problem, if not the sovereignty problem, at rest.

Partly as a result of these agreements and of the basic concurrence of the Philippines and the United States on international questions, the official policy of the Philippine government toward the United States was one of solid friendship throughout the term of the Magsaysay presidency (January 1954–March 1957).[13] In spite of this official policy, however, there was an increase in criticism of the United States, much of which was prompted by a growing spirit of nationalism. There was, as Meyer has noted, an intensification of "nationalist outbursts." These outbursts, he stated, took the form of criticism which

> embraced every major aspect of Philippine-American relations. They included questioning of the nature of existing trade relations, the scope of military bases, the delineation of jurisdiction on the bases, the extent of United States military assistance, the guarantees of United States military protection, and "subservient" alignment with the United States in international affairs.[14]

It would appear that as the Filipinos became more confident of their security and more conscious of their sovereignty they found themselves faced with a dilemma. On the one hand, they were anxious for increased United States commitments pertaining to economic and

[10] *New York Times*, September 26, 1951, p. 4. On a visit to the United States in June 1952, Ramon Magsaysay, who was to be elected President of the Philippines in 1953, stated that United States prestige in the Philippines had increased since independence. See *ibid.*, June 15, 1952, p. 4.

[11] See *ibid.*, October 28, 1952, p. 1. Among the specific matters discussed at this time, according to a communique, "was the role of the Philippines in the event of further Communist encroachment in Southeast Asia and the strengthening of United States bases in the Philippines to enable the United States to maximize its contribution to the defense of the Philippines and of Southeast Asia." As quoted in *ibid.*

[12] Southeast Asia Collective Defense Treaty. Signed at Manila September 8, 1954; entered into force for the United States February 19, 1955. 16 *UST* 81; *TIAS* 3170 (1955). The parties to the treaty are: Australia, France, New Zealand, Pakistan, the Philippines, Thailand, the United Kingdom, and the United States. For a discussion of the treaty, see George Modelski (ed.), *SEATO* (Melbourne: F. W. Cheshire, 1962).

[13] It should be pointed out that since World War II neither the question of the existence of United States bases in the Philippines nor the question of the status of the bases has ever been an issue dividing the two major parties, the Liberals and the Nationalistas.

[14] Meyer, p. 277.

security affairs, while on the other, their awakening concern with sovereignty called for a lessening of United States influence over both foreign and domestic policies. This desire for both security and sovereignty significantly influenced Filipino demands for revision of the criminal jurisdictional arrangements of the 1947 base agreement.

Presidential Overtures—First Attempts at Negotiation, 1953–1954

President Eisenhower made the initial move toward revision of the 1947 agreement in a letter to President Quirino, dated July 15, 1953, in which he spoke of increasing the number of active bases in the Philippines and further developing those bases which already were operating. In replying to President Eisenhower, President Quirino went beyond the suggestions of the Eisenhower letter when he said:

> I... share in your desire to reach an agreement on the questions concerning the military bases and other matters that remain unclarified or unresolved with a view to rendering more expeditiously effective our respective treaty undertakings insofar as these questions are concerned and to removing any possible cause for misunderstanding with regard to them.[15]

Apparently matters rested at this point until after the election of Ramon Magsaysay to the Presidency in late 1953.

In his first State of the Nation message of January 25, 1954, President Magsaysay stated:

> It is clearly in the national interest that we meet with the representatives of the United States Government to settle pending legal questions so that the bases we have granted to that country can be immediately developed and fully activated.[16]

Shortly thereafter he appointed a panel of Philippine negotiators to discuss issues with the United States.[17] This panel was headed by Vice-President Carlos Garcia, while the American panel was headed by Ambassador Raymond Spruance.[18] Apparently agreement was reached almost immediately on the nature of the ensuing talks. On March 15, the *New York Times* noted that the stage was set for negotiations concerning the questions of (1) sovereignty over the bases, (2) expansion of some bases, and (3) clarification of jurisdiction over the bases.[19]

On the next day United States Attorney General Brownell released a

[15] As quoted in Valeros, p. 20.
[16] Address on the State of the Nation by Ramon Magsaysay, January 25, 1954, 50 *Off. Gaz.* 81 (1954).
[17] *Manila Chronicle*, March 14, 1954, pp. 1, 3, as cited in Meyer, pp. 287–288.
[18] Arturo M. Tolentino, *Free Press*, February 13, 1965, p. 12.
[19] *New York Times*, March 15, 1954, p. 3.

legal opinion pertaining to the military reservations in the Philippines.[20] As Barrera has noted,

> the U.S. Attorney General stated that, with the exception of such military and naval properties "expressly and formally" conveyed to the Philippines, the United States retained title, "the proprietary interest as distinguished from sovereignty," to the land areas comprising: (1) the bases listed in Annexes A and B of the Military Bases Agreement [of 1947]; (2) the naval reservations and fueling stations not so listed in the Agreement; and (3) the areas covered by Article XXI of the same Agreement.[21]

The opinion by Brownell was based on the reservations in the proclamation of Philippine independence which stated that the proclamation was made "in accordance with and subject to the reservations provided for in the applicable statutes of the United States."[22]

According to Barrera, the disclosure of the Brownell opinion "generated a passionate reaction on the part of our government and people." Although Brownell had distinguished between "title" and "sovereignty," Barrera noted, this distinction, whatever may be its doctrinal standing, tends to be "insubstantial" on the "level of day-to-day realities," particularly where "land used and garrisoned by military forces is concerned."[23]

The Philippine panel immediately rejected this claim of United States ownership of the bases, and President Magsaysay postponed the talks.[24] According to Meyer, "Magsaysay took recourse to secret diplomatic negotiations to get title to the bases," and a period of two years passed before the resumption of formal talks.[25]

During this interim the United States, in the face of further Philippine criticism, continued the attempt to "allay any fears that the United States might not come to the aid of [the Philippines] in the event of aggression."[26] Apparently President Magsaysay was convinced

[20] See *Manila Chronicle*, March 17, 1954, pp. 1, 3, as cited inMeyer, p. 288. For the opinion of Attorney General Brownell to Secretary of State Dulles, dated August 28, 1953, see 41 *Op.A.G.* 143 (1963).

[21] Barrera, p. 643. See also Lorenzo Tanada, Jr., *Manila Sunday Times Magazine*, November 2, 1958, pp. 10–14.

[22] As quoted in Barrera, p. 644.

[23] *Ibid.*, pp. 643–644. See also Pacis, p. 31.

[24] Senator Claro Recto, a member of the panel, wrote the legal opinion refuting the United States claim. See Recto, *Philippine Herald*, May 10, 1954, p. 4. See also Tanjuakio, pp. 613–615; and Tolentino, *Free Press*, February 13, 1965, p. 12.

[25] Meyer, p. 289.

[26] *New York Times*, September 4, 1954, p. 3. Secretary of State Dulles stated that "the United States will honor fully its commitments under the mutual defense treaty. If the Philippines were attacked the United States would act immediately. We expect the Philippines to contribute to its own security to the extent of its capabilities. To that would be added the United States air, naval and logistical support." Dulles further noted that President Eisenhower had ordered the 7th Fleet to protect Formosa. "In the case of the Philippines," he stated, "no specific orders are required... Our forces would automatically react." As quoted in *ibid.*

of the sincerity of the United States commitment. In his State of the Nation message of January 1955, he stated that the United States had set forth a "categorical commitment of immediate assistance to our country in case of attack."[27] Although this increase in Philippine confidence was of importance, there was no agreement reached pertaining to the questions of sovereignty or clarification of jurisdiction on the bases.

Pelaez-Bendetsen Talks, 1956

On July 3, 1956, the occasion of the tenth anniversary of Philippine independence, President Magsaysay and Vice-President Nixon of the United States issued a joint statement in which it was stated that "the Philippines and the United States would resume negotiations on the military bases in the near future, and that the negotiations would be conducted on the basis of certain general principles," among which were the following:

> The United States has, since the independence of the Philippines, always acknowledged the sovereignty of the Philippines over such bases; and expressly reaffirms full recognition of such Philippine sovereignty over the bases. Further, the United States will transfer and turn over to the Philippines all title papers and title claims held by the United States to all land areas used either in the past or present as military bases, except those areas which may now or will be used by the United States for its diplomatic and consular establishments.[28]

This statement was followed in late July by the announcement that talks on the revision of the bases agreement would resume shortly.[29]

It is worthy of note that the composition of the negotiating panel which had been appointed by the Philippine government was distinctly different from that of the United States panel. With the exception of the Chief of Staff of the Armed Forces of the Philippines, all the mem-

[27] Address on the State of the Nation by President Magsaysay, January 24, 1955, 51 *Off. Gaz.* 103–104 (1955). Magsaysay further noted: "Actually, the United States military bases we now have here are America's earnest to us of automatic retaliation to aggression." *Ibid.* A few months after this statement Magsaysay asked the United States to reactivate certain idle military bases, because he realized "that these bases were vital to the defense of the Philippines in an atmosphere of growing world tension." As quoted in *New York Times*, May 11, 1955, p. 42. Magsaysay made it clear, however, that any new bases acquired by the United States would have a "leasehold status," thereby avoiding "the awkward question of United States ownership" which had been raised by Attorney General Brownell. *Ibid.*

[28] 35 *Department of State Bulletin* 95 (1956). See also *New York Times*, July 4, 1956, p. 1. Pascual and Majul attributed the turnover of the titles to the agitation of Senator Recto. Ricardo R. Pascual and Cesar A. Majul, *Foreign Policy of the Republic of the Philippines* (New York: Institute of Pacific Relations, 1957), p. 6. According to Meyer, Magsaysay's secret diplomatic negotiations had become a success by the middle of May. See Meyer, pp. 301–302.

[29] *New York Times*, July 22, 1956, p. 21.

bers of the Philippine panel were politicians. One of these politicians, Senator Emmanuel Pelaez, served as actual head of the panel.[30] The United States panel, on the other hand, was composed mainly of military officials with former Undersecretary of the Army Karl Bendetsen as actual head.[31] Obviously the Philippine government was giving the talks a political emphasis whereas the United States was placing the negotiations primarily in the hands of the Defense Department.[32]

Even before formal negotiations began the predominantly political interests of the Philippine panel were apparent. As early as May 25, Vice-President Garcia, the formal chairman-designate of the Philippine panel, released a proposed four-point agenda for the forthcoming talks. These points were: (1) jurisdiction within the bases; (2) delimitation and expansion of the bases; (3) taxes, tariffs, and other economic laws of the Philippines that the Philippines wanted to have applied to the bases; and (4) ownership and sovereignty over the bases.[33] During the weeks that followed there were numerous additional revisions and resolutions suggested by various Philippine senators and by a Special Committee of the Philippine House of Representatives.[34] Finally, three days prior to the opening of the formal talks, Garcia announced that the basic guidepost for the agenda would be the Nixon-Magsaysay joint statement of July 3. According to Garcia, the principles of main concern included: (1) the existence of the bases is a "matter of mutual interest and concern" for common defense; (2) the Philippines will grant new lands to the United States if it is mutually agreed that this is necessary, and the United States will turn over areas which it is mutually agreed are no longer necessary for mutual defense; and (3) the United States acknowledges sovereignty of the Philippines over the bases and will turn over the titles and claims of such bases to the Philippine government.[35]

The specific desires of the United States negotiators with respect to the talks are less well-known than those of the Philippine panel. How-

[30] See 52 *Off. Gaz.* ccclxxviii (1956). Vice-President and concurrently Secretary of Foreign Affairs Garcia was the formal chairman of the Philippine panel. *Ibid.*

[31] See Ambassador Albert F. Nufer's opening remarks at the plenary session of the bases talks, August 11, 1956, 52 *Off. Gaz.* 4583, 4584 (1956).

[32] See Taylor, pp. 237–238. Secretary of State Dulles later publicly stated that the negotiations were "primarily... in the hands of the Defense Department." *New York Times*, March 6, 1957, p. 4. For a similar statement by Dulles, see *ibid.*, November 20, 1957, p. 10.

[33] See *Manila Times*, May 26, 1956, p. 1, as cited in Meyer, p. 302.

[34] See Rafaelita Hilario-Soriano, "U.S.-P.I. Relations," *Progress Magazine 1956*, pp. 42–47, 216–218; Tolentino, *Free Press*, February 13, 1965, p. 44; Pascual and Majul, p. 28; *New York Times*, July 19, 1956, p. 12; Robert Alden, *ibid.*, July 30, 1956, p. 7; *Manila Times*, July 10, 1956, p. 1; and *ibid.*, July 11, 1956, p. 1.

[35] 52 *Off. Gaz.* ccclxiv (1956).

ever, it can be stated generally that the United States was primarily interested in modernizing the base system with respect to military matters.[36] The interests of both countries were evident in the final agenda announced in a joint statement by the Philippine and United States negotiators. This agenda included the following five areas:

1. Procedural matters.
2. Modernization of the bases system to provide common defense...
3. Working relationships and problems associated with the functioning of the bases [including] questions of commercial privileges and Philippine right to the exploitation of areas within the base reservations...
4. Problems associated with Philippine sovereignty, including the issue of jurisdiction within the reservations.
5. Correlation of the base system with the existing mutual defense treaty.[37]

The talks were formally opened by Vice-President Garcia on August 11, 1956.[38] In his opening remarks Garcia indicated that one major objective of the talks was to modernize the bases. He went on to say:

Of equal importance in our considered view, for insuring the utility of these bases for the purpose for which they have been established, are the negotiations aimed at eliminating all possible causes of misunderstanding between our two peoples and thus establish on firmer grounds the people's faith that, without prejudice to Philippine sovereignty and National dignity, the uses of these bases are common to the Philippines and the United States...[39]

In contrast, the opening statements of Ambassador Nufer and Karl Bendetsen seemed to indicate clearly that the United States conceived of the talks solely as a means of modernizing the bases and placed little emphasis on the second objective suggested by Garcia.[40] This basic difference in the conception of the purpose of the talks persisted throughout the negotiations.[41]

After the details of both the Philippine and the United States objectives were put forth, committees were formed to study specific ques-

[36] See *New York Times*, August 31, 1956, p. 3.

[37] *Ibid.*, August 8, 1956, p. 6.

[38] See 52 *Off. Gaz.* 4581, 4581–4583 (1956).

[39] *Ibid.*, p. 4581. See also Hilario-Soriano, p. 46.

[40] See Nufer's opening remarks at the plenary session of the bases talks, August 11, 1956, 52 *Off. Gaz.* 4583, 4583–4584 (1956); and Bendetsen's opening remarks..., *ibid.*, pp. 4584–4586. The opening statements by Garcia, Nufer, and Bendetsen are also reprinted in "The Military Bases Renegotiations Talks," 2 *Department of Foreign Affairs Review*, 53 (1956).

[41] See *New York Times*, August 31, 1956, p. 3; *ibid.*, December 6, 1956, p. 18; Tolentino, *Free Press*, February 13, 1965, p. 29; and Emilio Aguillar Cruz, "1956... Year of Nationalism," *Progress Magazine 1956*, pp. 18–25. See also the statement by Richard Nixon during the 1956 presidential election in the United States, where he stated that a central problem of the bases in the Philippines was that the Filipinos "have newly acquired their independence," and "they are very jealous of it and they do not want to have any infringement upon their sovereignty." As quoted in *New York Times*, October 5, 1956, p. 16. In the Philippine view, of course, the question of sovereignty was one of the major aspects of the causes of friction.

tions.[42] The issues discussed by the committee on sovereignty and jurisdiction, chaired by Undersecretary of Justice Barrera, are of primary concern to the present study.

The specific demands of the Filipino delegation on the issue of criminal jurisdiction were set forth by Barrera in a 1957 article which handled the jurisdictional question mainly in light of the necessity for Philippine sovereignty over the entire national territory of the Philippines.[43] In this connection, Barrera pointed out the three major proposals of the Philippine negotiators.

The first was related to the status of Olongapo, a barrio of some 60,000 inhabitants within the municipality of Subic, and at the same time within the Subic Bay Naval Reservation.[44] Barrera noted that in Olongapo, "the conduct and administrative control of civil affairs are in the hands, not of the duly elected municipal officials of Subic, but of United States naval officers."[45] Barrera stated that recently tensions had been developing inside and outside the reservation because of a number of "unfortunate incidents." He went on to say:

> The nature of military discipline and military organization, which is necessarily authoritarian even in the armed forces of democratic nations, often makes the exercise and observance of constitutionally guaranteed civil rights problematical and improbable in areas subject to military control and administration.

Because of such contradictions between military government and constitutional government, and because the Philippines were "anxious to remove once and for all this source of irritation and tension," the Philippine negotiators proposed that the administration and control of Olongapo be transferred to the Philippines.

The second concern of the Philippine panel was oriented toward the general question of United States jurisdiction over Filipinos.[46] Barrera noted that under the provisions of Article XIII, paragraph 1(a), of the 1947 agreement

> a citizen of the Philippines who commits an offense inside a base which is part of Philippine territory, may be tried by the military tribunals of [the United States] instead of the courts established by and provided for in the Constitution.

[42] For the specific objectives of the United States, insofar as they are known, see in particular *ibid.*, August 14, 1956, p. 8. For the Philippine objectives, see the speech of Senator Pelaez at the bases talks, August 15, 1956, 52 *Off. Gaz.* 4581, 4581–4605 (1956); and Hilario-Soriano, p. 216.

[43] Barrera, pp. 643–655. For a summary of the information revealed by Barrera in the *Decision Law Journal*, see Manuel Salak, *Manila Times*, July 15, 1958, pp. 1, 8.

[44] Unless otherwise noted, the following is drawn from Barrera, pp. 645–647.

[45] *Time* reported in July 1959 that Olongapo is "the only foreign city in the world run lock, stock, and barrel by the U.S. Navy." *Time*, July 20, 1959, p. 34. See also the editorial of the *Free Press*, July 18, 1959, p. 8.

[46] Unless otherwise noted, the following is drawn from Barrera, pp. 647–648.

No other published treaty, "outside the Soviet orbit," Barrera stated, allows for such trials of citizens of the receiving state by tribunals of the sending state.[47] He continued by saying:

It does not seem unreasonable to insist that a Filipino citizen has the legal right to be tried by a constitutional court of his own country within its own territory, and to the constitutionally ordained procedural safeguard which may not always be available in military courts whose proceedings are often summary in nature.

In order to remedy this "patently objectionable feature of the Military Bases Agreement" the Philippine negotiators proposed a provision

to the effect that "on no occasion and under no circumstances" may the United States military authorities "exercise jurisdiction" over a national or habitual resident of the Philippines who is not a member of the armed forces of the United States on active duty, or over any other person not a civilian component or a dependent.

The third objective of the Philippine delegation pertained to jurisdiction over the members of the United States armed forces, civilian component, and their dependents for offenses committed within the base areas.[48] According to Barrera, the Philippine negotiators recognized that "due regard must of necessity be given to the responsibilities of the military authorities in maintaining order and discipline inside the bases." For this reason the Philippine panel suggested

a compromise formula whereby jurisdiction will be assumed by the military authorities: (1) where the offender as well as the offended party is a member of the armed forces of the United States, a civilian component or a dependent; (2) where the offense is against the security of the United States; and (3) where the offense arose out of an act or omission done in the actual perfoımance of a specific military or official duty. The Philippine courts will take jurisdiction over a member of the armed forces, a civilian component or dependent only if the offense did not arise out of the actual performance of specific military or official duty and where the offended party is a Filipino citizen or habitual resident not a member of the armed forces and, additionally, only when the Secretary of Justice determines that it is of particular importance that the Philippines exercise jurisdiction over the case.

Thus the Philippine delegation apparently attempted to obtain an arrangement quite similar to that of the NATO Status of Forces Agreement (SOFA).

These three points put forth by the Philippine negotiators apparently were not completely acceptable to the United States panel. By August 23 it was reported that difficulties were arising, specifically over the jurisdictional question. As Hilario-Soriano has noted, the United States apparently "wanted to retain its extraterritorial rights over the

[47] As has been noted earlier the published treaties within the "Soviet orbit" do not provide for such trials. See above, chap. III, note 9.

[48] The following is drawn from Barrera, p. 648.

bases and have members of the United States armed forces charged with criminal offenses tried only by United States military authorities."[49] The Philippines argued that

> consistent with the recognition of sovereignty implied in the impending turnover of the titles to military reservations, all crimes within the bases should come under our jurisdiction except those involving Americans exclusively.[50]

According to the *Philippines Free Press*, the United States panel did indicate that it was willing to relinquish jurisdiction over Filipinos on the bases, but further agreement apparently was not possible at that time.[51]

In early September, after less than three weeks of negotiating, it was reported that an "impasse" had been reached in the negotiations "on the question of legal jurisdiction over personnel in military areas."[52] The most important question in dispute seemed to be who was to have jurisdiction over cases in which the offender in a criminal case was a member of the armed forces of the United States, the civilian component, or a dependent, and in which the offended party was not a member of the armed forces, the civilian component, or a dependent.[53] As the *New York Times* noted, the military bases in the Philippines

> employ thousands of Filipinos as clerks, laborers and domestic servants. Observers could envisage a demoralization of bases personnel if the Filipinos could invoke their own criminal laws against officers and enlisted men.[54]

Presumably the great fear of the United States negotiators was that large numbers of United States personnel would be subject to the jurisdiction of Philippine courts for offenses committed on the bases against nationals and habitual residents of the Philippines.

In early September the United States delegates indicated that the negotiations "would be broken off if the Filipinos maintained their insistence on the jurisdictional issue."[55] Since no progress was made in the weeks that followed, Bendetsen returned to the United States for instructions on September 25.[56] Upon his return to Manila on October 12, it was reported that the talks would be resumed.[57] Meyer stated, however, that the resumption of negotiations proved futile, and in order to save the talks, the two panels "agreed to tackle issues piecemeal, to

[49] Hilario-Soriano, p. 216.
[50] Cruz, p. 21.
[51] See Locsin, *Free Press*, October 27, 1956, p. 71.
[52] *New York Times*, September 4, 1956, p. 10.
[53] *Ibid.*, September 25, 1956, p. 3.
[54] *Ibid.*, September 4, 1956, p. 10.
[55] *Ibid.*
[56] *Manila Times*, September 25, 1956, p. 1; and *New York Times*, September 25, 1956, p. 3.
[57] *Free Press*, October 20, 1956, p. 69.

separate issues on which agreement was more likely from those where it was... [less likely]."[58] At least initially, this procedure seemed to meet with success. As Tolentino later reported, it was during this stage of the negotiations that complete agreement was reached on the turnover of a number of military and naval bases and the reduction of other bases. In addition, he noted, the panels came to agreement in principle on two other points: (1) the transfer of Olongapo to Philippine control; and (2) that "the United State military authorities would in no case exercise jurisdiction over a Philippine national or person habitually resident in the Philippines."[59] There were, however, some differences of opinion with regard to details on these two points.

Even while these negotiations were in progress it was reported in the United States that Bendetsen was preparing to leave the Philippines with his entire staff because of urgent business in Washington.[60] Tolentino noted that on December 5 "without previous warning and without asking the concurrence of the Philippine panel," the United States negotiators announced an "indefinite recess of the negotiations." "This," stated Tolentino, "was virtually the death-knell of those negotiations."[61] On December 8 the two panels disbanded, and apparently neither country made any official attempt to arrange for resumption of the talks at a later date.[62] Before leaving the country Bendetsen did turn over to the Philippines "all title papers and claims held by the United States to all land areas used as military bases."[63] This action, however, cannot be regarded as a result of the talks themselves since it already had been promised before the negotiations began in the Nixon-Magsaysay Joint Statement of July 3.

Two fundamental reasons may be cited for the lack of success of the 1956 negotiations.[64] The first of these is the apparently different points

[58] Meyer, pp. 307–308.

[59] Tolentino, *Free Press*, February 13, 1965, p. 32. See also *Manila Times*, December 1, 1956, p. 1.

[60] *New York Times*, November 26, 1956, p. 17.

[61] Tolentino, *Free Press*, February 13, 1965, p. 29. See also Meyer, p. 309; *New York Times*, December 6, 1956, p. 1; and *ibid.*, p. 3. Meyer maintained that the Philippines agreed that a recess was "compelling," but he cites no sources. None have been discovered by this writer.

[62] See Valeros, p. 22; Meyer, p. 411; and *Operation Hearings 1957*, p. 4.

[63] *New York Times*, December 6, 1956, p. 3. The total land area involved was 199,570 hectares. See 52 *Off. Gaz.* 7226, 7226–7227 (1956). Magsaysay cited this return of the title papers along with the rural development program as the major accomplishments of his administration in 1956. See 53 *Off. Gaz.* viii (1957). The United States retained title to: "(1) the United States Embassy and Chancery land in Manila; (2) 31 hectares in Baguio reserved in a diplomatic note prior to independence in 1946; (3) 10 hectares in Fort McKinley, subject to future negotiations." Meyer, p. 309.

[64] More would be known if the detailed report of the Philippine panel to President Magsaysay had been released. Magsaysay requested such a report, and it was received on

of view with which the two panels approached the talks. The United States negotiators, as Taylor noted, were only prepared to amend the 1947 agreement "so as to bring about the return of superfluous areas in exchange for new bases" and to facilitate the modernization of the bases. There was no idea of a complete overhaul of the agreement by the United States.[65] The Filipinos, on the other hand, used the opportunity to demand acceptance as an independent nation. As Pascual and Majul reported, the Philippine delegation and their demands were "motivated by the spirit of nationalism."[66] A reflection of this fundamental difference of approach by the two panels was the composition of the panels themselves. As was pointed out earlier, the United States negotiators were almost all military men while the Philippine panel was composed of political figures.

A second reason for the failure of the talks, as Taylor noted, was that "the negotiations were carried on more through press releases than by secret diplomacy."[67] Prior to the talks it was reported that the negotiations would take place in secret but that daily press briefings would be held.[68] Apparently a great deal of information was given out at these press briefings. According to Taylor,

> the result was that, once positions had been taken by either side, the possibility of compromise was seriously diminished. In this atmosphere reasonableness could easily be interpreted as weakness, and neither side was willing to make the first concession.[69]

President Magsaysay himself reportedly stated that one of the factors involved in the failure of the talks was "publicity." He is quoted as having said: "I should have handled it myself."[70]

Perhaps, as Tolentino has noted, one positive contribution made by the 1956 talks was the presentation of an opportunity for the "crystallization of the views and positions" of the two governments.[71] Prior to this time there had been no systematic attempt by the United States to obtain the specific views of the Filipinos relative to the bases. Having

March 3, 1957. Magsaysay stated that all portions of the report not concerned with Philippine national security, United States national security, or which would result in a breach of diplomatic protocol would be released. However, he had not decided what portions should be released before his death, and when Garcia became President, he stated that he would not release the report for publication. See 52 *Off. Gaz.* dciv (1956); 53 *Off. Gaz.* cvi–cxi (1957); and *ibid.*, clxx–clxxi (1957).

[65] Taylor, p. 238.
[66] Pascual and Majul, p. 6. See also Trumbull, *New York Times*, April 12, 1956, p. 6.
[67] Taylor, p. 238.
[68] *New York Times*, August 8, 1956, p. 6.
[69] Taylor, p. 238.
[70] Carlos Quirino, *Free Press*, October 26, 1957, p. 11, as cited in Meyer, p. 311.
[71] Tolentino, *Free Press*, February 13, 1965, p. 38.

obtained substantially advantageous provisions in the 1947 agreement, the United States was interested only in modernizing the bases and did not want to make basic alterations in the existing agreement. To the outside observer, however, it was becoming increasingly clear that if the bases were to contribute effectively to United States-Philippine security, they would have to be "modernized" not only with respect to contemporary weaponry, but also with respect to the working relationships in the functioning of the bases. The talks at least afforded the Filipinos the opportunity to show their concern with the latter aspect of the necessary modernization, even though no substantial agreements were reached as to how this should be accomplished.

Serrano-Bohlen Talks, 1958–1959

For almost two years following the breakdown of negotiations in December 1956 little was done to resume talks on the base issue. On several occasions the reopening of the talks was mentioned by President Garcia, but nothing ever materialized.[72] Although the United States made no attempt to resume negotiations, it did indicate its concern with the situation by appointing Charles E. Bohlen, one of its top diplomats, Ambassador to the Philippines in June 1957.[73] Within a year Bohlen had signed two important agreements. One relinquished United States control over the Manila Air Station,[74] and the other established a Philippine-United States Mutual Defense Board and provided for the assignment of Philippine military liaison officers to each

[72] In March 1957 Garcia said the talks had only been "recessed" and that "informal explorations" were being made through normal diplomatic channels concerning the resumption of the talks. He stressed, however, that the basis for the talks "must fall within the framework of the Philippine position." 53 *Off. Gaz.* cxliii (1957). A month later Garcia said he hoped the negotiations would be resumed. *Ibid.*, p. cxc (1957). He stated two months later that he did not think the talks would be resumed in 1957. *Ibid.*, p. cclxxviii (1957). Toward the middle of 1958 he "refused to comment on reports that the Philippines should take the initiative for the reopening of the bases talks with the U.S." 54 *Off. Gaz.* clxviii (1958).

During this two year period, in spite of numerous difficulties such as the Roe case in 1957 and the publicity of 1958–1959 involving the killings at Clark Field, the basic position of the Philippine government was staunchly pro-American. See in particular *New York Times*, April 28, 1957, p. 12; *ibid.*, November 19, 1957, p. 3; *ibid.*, January 27, 1959, p. 10; and 54 *Off. Gaz.* 315 (1958).

[73] See 53 *Off. Gaz.* cclxx–cclxxi (1957).

[74] The relinquishment of Manila Air Station occurred in two stages and actually involved two agreements. See Agreement Relating to the Immediate Release to the Philippine Authorities of Two Areas Occupied by the Manila Air Station (Exchange of notes at Manila January 27, 1958; entered into force January 27, 1958; 9 *UST* 131; *TIAS* 3985); and Agreement Relating to the Relinquishment to the Philippines of the Remaining Area of the Manila Air Station and the Deactivation of the Manila Air Base (Exchange of notes at Manila July 31, 1958; entered into force July 31, 1958; 9 *UST* 1075; *TIAS* 4083).

of the major United States military bases in the Philippines.[75] A *New York Times* editorial called the latter agreement a "quiet but significant gain" concerning the status of United States bases in the Philippines.[76] According to Rama, the establishment of the Military Liaison Officer within the bases "with some authority to decide or investigate cases involving Filipinos inside U.S. bases has removed a lot of misunderstanding."[77] Other important areas of disagreement, however, remained.

The beginning of what was to become substantial "understanding" on several of these issues came in July 1958 when Secretary of Justice Barrera urged that the Philippines take the initiative in reopening the talks on the bases.[78] In August it was reported that President Garcia "saw the 'need' to start exploratory talks along diplomatic channels in order to find a basis to resume the recessed panel discussions."[79] Apparently such a "basis" was found, as it was reported in late October that Ambassador Bohlen and Foreign Secretary Serrano had reached an agreement to begin talks on November 12.[80]

Little is known about the talks that took place. It is known, however, that Ambassador Bohlen returned to Washington in January 1959 and that the Philippine Ambassador to the United States, Carlos P. Romulo, was recalled to the Philippines, "apparently in reaction" to Bohlen's departure. At one point it was reported that Bohlen had returned to Washington to discuss the deteriorating United States-Philippine relations.[81] Later, however, it was reported that "lack of privacy was a factor in Mr. Bohlen's return to Washington for consultation..." The same source stated:

> After supposedly secret conferences with Foreign Secretary... Serrano, Mr. Bohlen found speculative accounts in Manila newspapers reporting with considerable accuracy what had taken place. He accused Mr. Serrano of tolerating leaks from his office.[82]

[75] Agreement for the Establishment of a Mutual Defense Board and the Assignment of Philippine Military Liaison Officers to United States Military Bases in the Philippines. Exchange of notes at Manila May 15, 1958; entered into force May 15, 1958. 9 *UST* 547; *TIAS* 4033.

[76] *New York Times*, May 20, 1958, p. 32.

[77] Rama, *Free Press*, December 26, 1964, p. 2. See also Tolentino, *ibid.*, February 13, 1965, p. 32.

[78] See Salak, *Manila Times*, July 15, 1958, p. 1.

[79] 54 *Off. Gaz.* ccxlii (1958).

[80] *New York Times*, October 29, 1958, p. 5.

[81] *Ibid.*, January 21, 1959, p. 6. See also *ibid.*, January 23, 1959, pp. 1, 8; *ibid.*, January 27, 1959, p. 10; *ibid.*, January 28, 1959, p. 6; and 40 *Department of State Bulletin* 224–225 (1959). For the issues involved in this deterioration, see Howard G. Glienke, "Irritants in P.I.-U.S. Relations," 3 *Kapisanang Pankasaysayan ng Pelipina* [Historical Bulletin] 60, 60–95 (1959). Apparently the basic factor involved was Philippine monetary claims against the United States, dating back to 1934, but primarily involving World War II damage claims.

[82] *New York Times*, March 6, 1959, p. 2.

Whatever the cause of his departure from the Philippines, Ambassador Bohlen returned to Manila in late February after a five weeks absence.[83] Shortly thereafter he and President Garcia, with Secretary Serrano present, reportedly agreed that all future talks would be "in strict privacy at times and places unannounced beforehand or afterwards."[84]

As Tolentino noted, the subsequent talks between Serrano and Bohlen "were called 'exploratory,' in the sense that whatever agreements might be reached... should be regarded as tentative and recommendatory in character."[85] Out of these "exploratory" talks came one formal agreement and two memorandums of agreement. The agreement was a legal international obligation of the United States. The two memorandums did not purport to be formal agreements "creating obligations between the two governments," but rather "interim understandings with respect to matters to be included" in formal agreements at a later date.[86]

The first memorandum of agreement, announced on August 4, 1959, called for the relinquishing to the Philippines of seventeen base areas with a total area of over 117,075 hectares.[87] These areas were to be relinquished by the United States "in return for [the] designation of certain areas as 'integral parts' of adjoining United States bases."[88] Thus an understanding had been achieved regarding one of the Philippine goals, the obtaining of unused areas and base areas not necessary for mutual defense. At the same time, the United States military was to obtain areas that it felt were necessary for improving the military efficiency of the remaining bases. This memorandum of agreement was formalized and put into effect on December 22, 1965.[89]

[83] *Ibid.*, February 20, 1956, p. 6. See also *ibid.*, February 25, 1959, p. 15.

[84] *Ibid.*, March 6, 1959, p. 2.

[85] Tolentino, *Free Press*, February 13, 1965, p. 29. This report is confirmed at 55 *Off. Gaz.* 985 (1959); and *ibid.*, p. clxviii (1959).

[86] Personal letter from Mr. Eugene T. Herbert, Attorney, Office of the Legal Adviser, Department of State, dated June 20, 1966.

[87] This memorandum of agreement is reprinted in 3 *PILJ* 438, 438–442 (1964). Of the seventeen bases, "nine were [to be] relinquished absolutely and completely, four were [to be] relinquished subject to their availability for combined PI-US operational use in case of military necessity, and four others were [to be] relinquished partially and subject to some specified conditions." Tolentino, *Free Press*, February 13, 1965, p. 38.

[88] *New York Times*, August 19, 1959, p. 6.

[89] Agreement Relating to the Relinquishment and the Acquisition of Certain Base Lands in the Philippines by the United States, with Annex. Exchange of notes at Manila December 22, 1965; entered into force December 22, 1965. *TIAS*, 5924. The United States now retains three major bases in the Philippines—the naval bases at Subic Bay and Sangley Point and the air base at Clark Field—and a military recreational center at Baguio—Camp John Hay. In addition to these bases, a few minor installations, such as communication centers, are retained.

On October 12, 1959, a second "understanding" was announced.[90] This memorandum of agreement stated:

In accordance with the understanding reached during our discussions in August, September, and October, 1959, the following is agreed:

(a) Consultations: The operational use of United States bases in the Philippines for military combat operations, other than those conducted in accordance with the United States-Philippines Mutual Defense Treaty and the Southeast Asian Collective Defense Treaty will be the subject of prior consultation with the Government of the Philippines. The establishment by the United States of long-range missiles (IRBM, ICBM) on United States bases in the Philippines will be the subject of prior consultation with the Government of the Philippines.

(b) Duration and termination: ...[The duration of the Military Bases Agreement of 1947 is reduced from 90 to 25 years with a] proviso for renewal at the expiration of the 25 year period or earlier termination by mutual agreement. [The 25 year period begins on date of signature].

(c) Mutual Defense: ...[The policy of the United States with regard to armed attack on the Philippines] is contained in the Mutual Defense Treaty. Further the United States reaffirms the policy set forth in the statement of September 7, 1954 of then Secretary of State Dulles... and in the joint communique issued on June 20, 1959 by President Eisenhower and President Garcia... [where it was stated that President Eisenhower had "made clear" that] any armed attack against the Philippines would involve an attack against United States forces stationed there and against the United States and would instantly be repelled.[91]

The formal agreement reached during the Serrano-Bohlen talks concerned the question of Olongapo. Olongapo, as has been noted, was located within the confines of the Subic Bay Naval Base and was administered by the United States Navy, a situation which had stimulated serious conflict between the United States and the Philippines. An agreement was reached on December 7, 1959, to change the base limits of Subic Bay Naval Station to exclude Olongapo.[92]

Thus during the period in which Bohlen was ambassador three major steps were taken to make the defense relationship between the United States and the Philippines more mutual. Although only one formal agreement was reached, the "intentions" of the United States in the two memorandums were accepted by the Filipinos as satisfactory re-

[90] This memorandum of agreement is reprinted in 3 *PILJ* 442, 442–445 (1964); and in Locsin, *Free Press*, October 17, 1959, p. 74. An account of the memorandum can also be found in Wilkins, *New York Times*, October 13, 1959, p. 1.

[91] 3 *PILJ* 442, 442–444 (1964). Although this understanding was not formalized immediately, it has been noted that "the language contained in the Memorandum concerning mutual defense is... a unilateral statement of United States policy." Personal letter from Mr. Herbert, dated June 20, 1966. While this study was in its final stages of preparation, Secretary of Foreign Affairs Ramos and Secretary of State Rusk, in an exchange of notes dated September 16, 1966, formalized the agreements reached in the memorandum of October 12, 1959. See 55 *Department of State Bulletin* 548 (1966).

[92] Agreement Relating to the Relinquishment of Olongapo and Adjacent Areas, with Annex. Exchange of notes at Manila December 7, 1959; entered into force December 7, 1959. 10 *UST* 2169; *TIAS* 4388.

sponses to several of the demands they had set forth during the 1956 talks. When the memorandum of agreement of October 12 was announced, Locsin, one of the more vocal critics of United States policy in the Philippines, stated: "Never has Philippine sovereignty seemed so real!"[93] President Garcia himself, on the occasion of Bohlen's departure from the Philippines for a change of posts to Washington, stated that the issue of the bases involved most delicate questions and that in less capable hands than Bohlen's, the friendship between the Philippines and the United States might have been "imperiled." The President pointed to the agreement and the memorandums mentioned above as major accomplishments in United States-Philippine relations during Bohlen's tour of duty, but apparently of more importance to him was the fact that Bohlen had publicly recognized "the legitimacy of nationalism in the Philippines."[94]

In spite of abundant Philippine praise for Bohlen's accomplishments one very important general complaint of the Philippines remained. This was the question of criminal jurisdiction. On several occasions during the talks it was reported that Bohlen and Serrano were approaching a final decision concerning this question, but apparently no real progress was made.[95]

Mendez-Blair Talks, 1965

After Ambassador Bohlen departed from the Philippines there were a few unsuccessful attempts to revise the criminal jurisdictional arrangements.[96] By the end of 1960, however, the issue apparently was attracting little attention. This was true until November 1964, when the incident at Clark Field involving the killing of Rogelio Balagtas by Airman Cole occurred, followed closely by the Gonzalo Villedo killing at Subic Bay by Corporals Edwards and Thomas. Once again there was an outcry of public indignation. According to one report, "tempers" ran high and

> Filipino leaders and the press unanimously demanded the immediate resumption of negotiations with the United States to modify the 1947 treaty on military bases and

[93] Locsin, *Free Press*, October 10, 1959, pp. 3, 67.
[94] 55 *Off. Gaz.* cdxxx–cdxxxi (1959). See also *New York Times*, October 15, 1959, p. 11.
[95] See Locsin, *Free Press*, April 4, 1959, p. 3; *New York Times*, May 14, 1959, p. 4; *Time*, July 20, 1959, p. 34; Locsin, *Free Press*, August 8, 1959, p. 3; *ibid.*, October 10, 1959, p. 3; Wilkins, *New York Times*, October 13, 1959, p. 1; *Free Press*, October 17, 1959, p. 8.
[96] See 56 *Off. Gaz.* ccxlvii (1960); *New York Times*, September 22, 1960, p. 5; and *ibid.*, November 30, 1960, p. 17.

to give Philippine courts jurisdiction over offenses committed on American bases on the islands against Filipino nationals.[97]

Within a few days after the second killing President Macapagal held a cabinet meeting to discuss the killings and afterwards announced that the Foreign Office had been ordered to resume the efforts to revise the jurisdictional arrangements set forth in the 1947 agreement. Shortly thereafter, a government investigation was begun.[98] Before the end of December demonstrations had been held protesting the killings; demands for the recall of Ambassador Blair had been voiced by Philippine politicians, civic groups, and bar associations; the personnel and their families at Clark Field had been restricted to the base for their protection on one occasion; and there had been some demand for the removal of United States bases from the Philippines.[99] Against this background Foreign Secretary Mendez and United States Ambassador Blair started "exploratory" talks in early January 1965 aimed at revising the agreement.[100]

Included in Rama's report of the beginning of the talks was a list of some basic guidelines designed to obtain a compromise solution which had been offered by former Foreign Secretary Serrano. Serrano stated:

1. American military bases exist in the Philippines, by our consent, to enable the United States to more effectively discharge its responsibility of defending our country against aggression, under the Mutual Defense Pact. Undeniably the subtraction of our sovereign rights, to the extent they are pre-empted in the corresponding exercise of American jurisdiction, is the price we have agreed to pay to better safeguard our national security.

2. As the exercise of American jurisdiction is a derogation and subtraction *pro tanto* of our sovereign rights within our territory it should practically be limited to every possible but unavoidable minimum; beyond this minimum, the majesty of our laws and sovereignty must be held supreme.

3. In the twilight cases, where both principles apply in varying degree, suitable arrangements on concurrent exercise, or reciprocal waiver, of jurisdiction must be worked out with respectful regard to where lie the superior interests of one country or the other.[101]

Serrano, thus, was suggesting something similar to the criminal jurisdictional provisions of the NATO SOFA. In fact, Rama concluded his article by noting that in view of Serrano's approach "perhaps a lot of

[97] *Ibid.*, December 25, 1964, p. 10. See also Rama, *Free Press*, December 26, 1964, p. 2.

[98] *Ibid.*

[99] See *New York Times*, December 25, 1964, p. 10; *ibid.*, December 26, 1964, p. 2; Rama, *Free Press*, December 26, 1964, p. 2; and *New York Times*, December 28, 1964, p. 13.

[100] Rama, *Free Press*, January 9, 1965, p. 7; see also Trumbull, *New York Times*, January 6, 1964, p. 4. In reporting the beginning of the negotiations, Trumbull stated that the jurisdictional problem has "darkened" United States-Philippine relations periodically since 1946. *Ibid.*

[101] As quoted in Rama, *Free Press*, January 9, 1965, p. 7.

bitterness, waste of time and effort could be avoided by merely asking the American government to grant us the same concessions it was willing to give to other countries."[102] Apparently this was the path the negotiations followed.

In early February it was reported that Ambassador Blair had offered the Philippines broader jurisdiction.[103] Reportedly, this offer went far toward meeting the "clamor" for a revision which had been raised by the Philippine press.[104] By May the negotiators apparently had reached agreement on the question of jurisdiction. [105] Finally, on August 10, 1965, a new executive agreement between the United States and the Philippines was signed.[106] This new agreement went into effect immediately without being submitted for approval to either the United States Senate or the Philippine Senate.

[102] *Ibid.*, p. 72.
[103] *New York Times*, February 5, 1965, p. 2.
[104] *Ibid.*
[105] See Seth King, *ibid.*, May 23, 1965, p. 23.
[106] It should be noted that little publicity was given to the Mendez-Blair talks, and no further information is available. Apparently, these talks, like the successful Bohlen-Serrano talks, were conducted in strict privacy. See 53 *Department of State Bulletin* 358 (1965).

CHAPTER VI

CRIMINAL JURISDICTIONAL ARRANGEMENTS UNDER THE 1965 AGREEMENT

The criminal jurisdictional arrangements of the 1965 agreement were aimed at eliminating one of the most serious irritants in United States-Philippine relations.[1] United States Ambassador Blair called it "a fair and equitable arrangement,"[2] and the *Manila Times* reported that it "appears so logical an arrangement that one wonders why it took so long to negotiate."[3] Perhaps the twelve years of intermittent negotiations are the best testimony to the serious and sensitive nature of the conflicts involved. Although many of these problems still exist, the new agreement provides a better basis for handling them. At the same time, however, as is the case with any new arrangement, the 1965 agreement poses potential operational problems of its own.

The following discussion will attempt to describe the content of the agreement including the attached Agreed Official Minutes and Agreed Implementing Arrangements, the conflicts it settled, and those it may produce. Where appropriate, the new arrangements will be compared with the original Article XIII of the 1947 agreement, the NATO Status of Forces Agreement (SOFA), and other status of forces agreements.

The 1965 revision of Article XIII of the 1947 agreement is almost identical to the criminal jurisdictional provisions of Article VII of the NATO SOFA.[4] Thus the United States-Philippine agreement seems to

[1] Agreement Relating to Criminal Jurisdiction Arrangement, Amending the Agreement of March 14, 1947, as Amended. Exchange of notes at Manila August 10, 1965; entered into force August 10, 1965. 16 *UST* 1090; *TIAS* 5851. Offenses committed before the provisions of the revised agreement came into effect will be governed by the provisions of the original Article XIII (Agreed Official Minute Number 8). For the instructions to the military authorities in the Philippines putting the revised agreement into effect, see CINCPAC Representative Philippines and Commander, U.S. Naval Forces Philippines, *CINCPACREP PHIL/COMNAVPHIL Instruction 5820.1B*, dated September 7, 1965.

[2] As quoted in *Free Press*, August 21, 1965, p. 91.

[3] Maximo V. Soliven, *Manila Times*, August 12, 1965, p. 5-A.

[4] Except for some changes in terminology necessitated by the different parties to the agreement and other changes which are apparently of no importance, the formal amendment is in complete agreement with the provisions of Article VII of the NATO SOFA even as to paragraph numbers through paragraph 9(f). Paragraph 9(g) of the NATO SOFA provides that a representative of the sending state may be present at the trial of an accused who is

fulfill the Philippine desires to have the United States treat it as it does other countries. Closer examination, however, reveals significant differences between the United States-Philippine arrangements and the United States arrangements with the NATO countries. The Agreed Official Minutes and Agreed Implementing Arrangements which are attached to the new agreement impose numerous qualifications on much of what is stated in the revision of Article XIII per se. The nature of these qualifications, which seem to take away some of what the revised article provides, are of major importance in interpreting the new agreement itself and in comparing it with other status of forces agreements, including the 1947 United States-Philippine agreement.

General Principles of Jurisdiction

According to paragraph 1(a) the Philippine authorities have jurisdiction over all members of the United States armed forces or civilian component and their dependents "with respect to offenses committed within the Republic of the Philippines and punishable by the law of the Republic of the Philippines." Paragraph 1(b) provides that the United States military authorities have the "right to exercise" within the Philippines "all criminal and disciplinary jurisdiction" conferred on them by the law of the United States over all persons subject to the military law of the United States.[5]

Under Article 2 of the Uniform Code of Military Justice (U.C.M.J.), it is specified that in addition to ordinary personnel the Code applies to "persons serving with, employed by, or accompanying the armed forces" outside the United States, subject to the provisions of treaties,

subject to the provisions of the agreement "when the rules of court permit." Since no such qualification is included in the Philippine agreement, presumably a representative could always be present at trial proceedings in the Philippines.

No discussion of the civil jurisdictional arrangements will be made in this chapter. The new agreement, in the exchange of notes putting the agreement into effect, specifies that paragraph 8 of the original Article XIII will continue in effect. Thus the provisions of Article XIII, paragraph 8 and Article XXIII continue as the bases for processing civil claims. Insofar as is known these provisions have caused no difficulties.

[5] As Baldwin has pointed out, it is important to note that status of forces agreements concern the "right to exercise" criminal jurisdiction and not the existence of jurisdiction. Baldwin, p. 61. Thus under both the original and revised versions of Article XIII, it is not the existence of the United States military authorities' jurisdiction over persons subject to the military law of the United States that is recognized, but rather the right of the United States authorities to exercise this jurisdiction in the Philippines. Without such an agreement, as Baldwin noted, a United States court-martial could not sit in the host country without infringing on the rights of that country. *Ibid.* See also *The S.S. "Lotus"* (France v. Turkey), *PCIJ* 1927, Ser. A., No. 10, 2 Hudson, *World Court Reports* 20 (1935), and *Schooner Exchange* v. *McFaddon,* 7 Cranch (U.S.) 116, 136 (1812), as cited in William W. Bishop, Jr., *International Law* (2d ed. rev.; Boston: Little, Brown, and Co., 1962), pp. 443, 448.

agreements, and accepted rules of international law.[6] In a series of cases from 1957–1960, however, the United States Supreme Court declared that Congress does not have the power to subject civilians to court-martial jurisdiction in times of peace.[7] As Duke and Vogel pointed out, the Supreme Court decisions

> can be viewed as logical, albeit far-reaching extensions of basic constitutional doctrine that persons who are not actually in the armed forces are not to be deprived of the rights guaranteed to them by the Constitution.[8]

As might be expected, there was considerable speculation as to the adverse effect these rulings might have on overseas bases. Such speculations ranged from the view that there would be wholesale criminal violations by employees, and dependents, with the accompanying disciplinary problems, to the fear of "harsh investigatory, confinement, and trial procedures" that allegedly are found in many foreign coun-

[6] See 64 *Stat.* 107 (1950); 10 *U.S.C.* 801, Article 2, paragraphs 10 and 11. As Rouse and Baldwin have noted: "This has been construed to confer military jurisdiction over civilian employees of United States nationality of both appropriated [citing *U.S.* v. *Monker*, 1 *U.S.C.M.A.* 393, 3 *C.M.R.* 127] and non-appropriated fund activities (such as officer's clubs, post exchanges and Armed Forces Picture Service) [citing *U.S.* v. *Biagini* 10 *C.M.R.* 682, 690], certain merchant seamen [citing *U.S.* v. *Garcia*, 5 *U.S.C.M.A.* 88; 17 *C.M.R.* 88], aliens brought within a receiving state as employees [citing *U.S.* v. *Weiman*, 3 *U.S.C.M.A.* 216, 11 *C.M.R.* 216], technical representatives of contractors serving with the forces [citing *Perlstein* v. *U.S.*, 151 F. 2d 167 (3rd Cir., 1945); cert. dismissed, 328 U.S. 822 (1946); *In re Di Bartalo*, 50 F. Supp. 929 (SDNY, 1943)]..." Joseph H. Rouse and Gordon B. Baldwin, "The Exercise of Criminal Jurisdiction Under the NATO Status of Forces Agreement," 51 *AJIL* 29, 33 (1957). Article 2 has also been applied to dependents of members of the armed forces and of the civilian component accompanying them by military authorization. See Lewis Mayers, *The American Legal System* (rev. ed.; New York: Harper and Brothers, 1964), p. 511.

[7] On rehearing *Reid* v. *Covert* and a companion case, *Kinsella* v. *Kruger*, 354 U.S. 1 (1957), the Court reversed its original ruling (*Reid* v. *Covert*, 351 U.S. 487, 1956; *Kinsella* v. *Kruger* 351 U.S. 470, 1956) and ordered released two military dependents charged with murder. In both cases the alleged crimes had been committed overseas, and the women had been tried by courts-martial under Article 2, section 11 of the U.C.M.J. In the *Covert* ruling, however, no explicit statement was made as to whether it applied to non-capital cases. In January 1960 the questions unanswered in the *Covert* case were handled in four Supreme Court cases. The Court held that courts-martial "cannot constitutionally exercise jurisdiction over persons who do not have a 'status' as members of the armed forces." Robert D. Duke and Howard S. Vogel, "The Constitution and the Standing Army: Another Problem of Court-Martial Jurisdiction," 13 *Vanderbilt Law Review* 435, 437 (1960). See also *Operation Hearings 1960*, pp. 2–3. For civilian dependents accused of non-capital offenses, see *Kinsella* v. *United States ex rel. Singleton*, 361 U.S. 234 (1960). For civilian employees charged with capital offenses, see *Grisham* v. *Hagen*, 361 U.S. 278 (1960). For civilian employees accused of non-capital offenses, see *McElroy* v. *United States ex rel. Guagliardo* and *Wilson* v. *Bohlender* 361 U.S. 281 (1960). It should be pointed out that these decisions did not involve "petty offenses." Thus, as a Defense Department official has noted, it is not clear whether the' Supreme Court decisions "really applied to [court-martial jurisdiction over] petty offenses.' The same official stated, however, that the military has not tried any such case since the Supreme Court rulings. *Operation Hearings 1965*, p. 15.

[8] Duke and Vogel, p. 437. See also John C. Reis and Owen S. Nibley, "Justice, Juries, and Military Dependents," 15 *Western Political Quarterly* 438, 440–441 (1962).

ties.[9] In response to these opinions there were numerous unsuccessful attempts, many of them in the form of proposed constitutional amendments, to reinstate military court-martial jurisdiction.[10] The reason for their failure may have been that there was no indication of an increase in offenses by civilian employees and dependents after the Supreme Court rulings.[11] Moreover, the Department of Defense stated that the commanders in the field reported "no adverse effects upon the morale of their personnel or upon the accomplishment of their mission from our present inability to try civilians by court-martial."[12] This absence of a negative influence of the Supreme Court decisions may have been due, at least in part, to the substantial amount of control the military still could exercise over civilian employees and dependents. As noted in Chapter IV, this is administrative control in the form of dismissal or suspension of employment, withholding or denying certain privileges on base such as post exchange privileges, the right to drive on base, etc., and returning dependents to the United States while the military or civilian employee stays on unaccompanied by his dependents.[13]

Although the consequences of the Supreme Court rulings were not as extreme as speculations had suggested, many Filipinos were not satisfied with the situation. Typical of these was Valeros, who stated:

> Since an American Supreme Court decision ruled that American military authorities can no longer try these civilian dependents during peace-time, the Philippines may exercise jurisdiction over the offense that may be committed by these civilians without waiting for the military authorities to waive the jurisdiction they no longer have. Unless a new arrangement on this point is reached American civilian offenders may go unpunished and a new source of misunderstanding added.[14]

Under the new agreement this criticism by Valeros is met. Agreed Official Minute Number 1 explicitly recognizes the fact that contemporary United States law, as set forth by the Supreme Court, exempts

[9] See *ibid.*, pp. 438–448; and *Operation Hearings 1956*, p. 12. Reis and Nibley, two officers in the United States Air Force, maintain that "there is simply no solution [to the problem] short of re-establishing court-martial jurisdiction." Reis and Nibley, p. 444.

[10] For the courses of action possible to regain military jurisdiction over civilians, see *ibid.*, pp. 438–448; *Operation Hearings 1960*; *Operation Hearings 1961*; and Thomas B. Moorhead, "*Reid* v. *Covert* and Its Progeny: The Practical Problem of Punishment," 12 *Syracuse Law Review* 18, 18–25 (1960).

[11] See *Operation Hearings 1964*, p. 5. From data available to the author it appears that there have been only three trials of civilians by the Philippine courts from 1954 through 1964. One trial of a member of the civilian component occurred in 1959. Two trials of dependents occurred in 1964, but the lack of any such cases from 1960 through 1963 seems to indicate that the Supreme Court rulings are not the determining variable. Drawn from *OCS Form 782*, Philippines (1954–1955) and *JAG Form 66* [replaces *OCS Form 782*], Philippines (1956–1964).

[12] *Operation Hearings 1962*, pp. 2, 22. See also *Operation Hearings 1960*, p. 3.

[13] See above, pp. 64–65, and *Operation Hearings 1964*, p. 4.

[14] Valeros, p. 25.

civilians from court-martial jurisdiction in times of peace. Thus the Philippines necessarily has the primary right to exercise jurisdiction over United States civilians. In order to clarify this completely, Agreed Minute Number 1, referring specifically to the Supreme Court rulings, states:

> The term "persons subject to the military law of the United States" does not apply to members of the civilian component or dependents, with respect to whom there is no effective military jurisdiction at the time this arrangement enters into force.

In order to minimize any future difficulties concerning this issue, it further states that if the coverage of court-martial jurisdiction should change by constitutional amendment or otherwise, the United States shall notify the Philippines through diplomatic channels. Presumably this means that there would be no conflict if, in the future, the provisions of the United States law should change.

Paragraph 4 of the new agreement specifically states that the United States shall under no circumstances have the right to exercise jurisdiction over Philippine nationals or persons "ordinarily resident" in the Philippines, "unless they are members of the United States armed forces." This provision represents one of the most significant differences between the original jurisdictional arrangements and the revised Article XIII and brings the United States-Philippine agreement into line with other status of forces agreements, a goal which the Philippines had been eager to attain.

To facilitate the handling of conflicts which might arise under the provisions of the revised agreement, Agreed Implementing Arrangement Number 4 provides for the establishment of a Criminal Jurisdiction Implementation Committee. The Committee is to be organized so as to be able to "meet promptly at any time upon the request of either of the two governments." Any matter which the Committee is unable to resolve "shall be referred to the respective governments for further consideration."

Exclusive Jurisdiction

Paragraph 2(a) provides that the Philippine authorities have "exclusive jurisdiction" over United States armed forces or their civilian components and their dependents in cases of offenses punishable by the law of the Philippines but not punishable by the law of the United States.[15] Similarly the United States authorities, under the provisions of

[15] It would be extremely difficult for the Philippines to claim exclusive jurisdiction over

paragraph 2(b), have the exclusive right to exercise jurisdiction over persons subject to the military law of the United States with respect to offenses punishable by the law of the United States, including offenses against the security of the United States, but not punishable by the law of the Philippines.[16]

These provisions are the same as those of the NATO SOFA and the United States-Japanese agreement. They appear, however, to differ from the provisions of the Soviet agreements with East Germany, Hungary, and Poland. None of the Soviet agreements refer to "exclusive" jurisdiction, and any offense over which both the Soviet Union and the receiving state have jurisdiction is subject to waiver.[17] Presumably, if an offense were punishable by the law of only one of the parties to the agreement, that state would have exclusive jurisdiction since the other state would have no forum under which it could exercise jurisdiction.

It should be pointed out that in the United States-Philippine agreement the provision of paragraph 6 of the original Article XIII, which granted the United States exclusive jurisdiction over its armed forces in time of war, continues in effect under the provision of Agreed Official Minute Number 6 of the revised agreement.

Concurrent Jurisdiction

In all cases other than those covered by paragraphs 2(a) and 2(b), the right to exercise criminal jurisdiction is concurrent. Paragraph 6(b) provides that the two states notify "one another of the disposition of all cases in which there are concurrent rights to exercise jurisdiction." Presumably this provision will mitigate the possibility of disputes arising out of flagrant violations of justice by either state not prosecuting obvious criminal cases.

The arrangements for determining which authority has the primary right to exercise jurisdiction in cases of concurrent jurisdiction are found

persons subject to the military law of the United States under paragraph 2(a) because of the fact that Article 134 of the U.C.M.J. prohibits "all conduct of a nature which may bring discredit upon the armed forces." Rouse and Baldwin, p. 38. See also Note, 70 *Harvard Law Review* 1043, 1056 (1957); and de Castro, p. 936. For the vagueness of Article 134, see Robert O. Everett, "Article 134, Uniform Code of Military Justice—A Study in Vagueness," 37 *North Carolina Law Review* 142, 142–161 (1958).

[16] Paragraph 2(c) points out that for the purpose of paragraphs 2 and 3 security offenses include "(i) Treason against the State [and] (ii) Sabotage, espionage or violation of any law relating to official secrets of that State, or secrets relating to the national defense of that State."

[17] See 52 *AJIL* 212, 217–218, 224 (1958).

in the paragraphs of section 3. Paragraph 3(a) provides that the Philippines has the primary right to exercise jurisdiction in all cases not set forth in paragraph 3(b). Under the provisions of paragraph 3(b) the United States has the primary right to exercise jurisdiction over all persons subject to the military law of the United States in relation to:

(i) offenses solely against the property or security of the United States, or offenses solely against the person or property of a member of the United States armed forces or civilian component or of a dependent.
(ii) offenses arising out of any act or omission done in the performance of official duty.

In an attempt to eliminate difficulties of interpretation, the meaning of "official duty" is explained in Agreed Minute Number 2. According to Minute Number 2,

official duty is not meant to include all acts by an individual during the period while he is on duty, but is meant to apply only to acts which are required or authorized to be done as a function of that duty which the individual is performing.

It is understood to be "any duty or service required or authorized to be done by statute, regulation, the order of a superior or military usage." Agreed Minute Number 3 further provides that in cases where it is necessary to determine whether or not an

alleged offense arose out of an act or omission done in the performance of official duty, a certificate issued by or on behalf of the commanding officer of the alleged offender or offenders, on advice of the Staff Legal Officer or Staff Judge Advocate, will be delivered promptly to the city or provincial fiscal (prosecuting attorney) concerned, and this certificate will be honored by the Philippine authorities.

Where the military certificate is "questioned" by the fiscal, Minute 3 states that it shall be made a subject of "discussions between appropriate officials of the Government of the Republic of the Philippines and the diplomatic mission of the United States," as long as a request is received by the United States mission within ten days from receipt of the certificate by the fiscal. This is the only part of the new agreement that offers the possibility of an increase in United States jurisdiction as compared with its jurisdiction under the 1947 provisions. The original Article XIII gave the Philippine authorities the final determination as to whether or not an offense occurred in the performance of official duty. Obviously the new agreement constitutes a significant change relative to this aspect of the question of official duty.

It should be noted that according to Minute Number 1, the primary jurisdiction of the United States is extended "only to those persons subject to the military law of the United States regularly assigned to the Philippines or present in the Philippines in connection with the presence there of the U.S. bases." Thus, the jurisdictional provisions of the Philippine agreement, unlike the agreement with Japan, do not cover military personnel on leave status who are not stationed in the receiving state.[18] It appears, however, that the provisions of the Philippine agreement would cover United States personnel stopping over at the bases temporarily in connection with a military mission elsewhere. Presumably such personnel would be "present in the Philippines in connection with the presence there of the U.S. bases."

Waiver of Jurisdiction

As is provided in the NATO SOFA, paragraph 3(c) of the United States-Philippine agreement indicates that if the state with the primary right to exercise jurisdiction decides not to exercise that right in any particular case, it shall notify the other party "as soon as practicable." The same paragraph further provides that the state with the primary right to exercise jurisdiction shall give "sympathetic consideration" to requests from the other party for a waiver "of its right in cases where that other State considers such waiver to be of particular importance." Paragraphs 3(a) and 3(c), however, are supplemented by Agreed Official Minute Number 4 which sets the stage for waiver provisions which are significantly different from those under the NATO SOFA. Minute Number 4 first recognizes that the maintenance of "good order and discipline" of those subject to United States military law is primarily the responsibility of the United States authorities. It goes on to say that the Philippines agrees to "waive their primary right to exercise jurisdiction under paragraph 3(a)," when requested by the United States authorities, "except where they determine that it is of particular importance that jurisdiction be exercised by the Philippine authorities."[19] The United States, as can be seen, must take positive action in

[18] For the Japanese provision, see Article I, paragraph a, Agreement of January 19, 1960, *TIAS* 4510.

[19] Other arrangements which include waiver provisions similar to those of the United States-Philippine agreement include Greece (Agreement of September 7, 1956; 7 *UST* 2555; *TIAS* 3649), Nicaragua (Agreement of September 5, 1958; 9 *UST* 1206; *TIAS* 4106), the Federation of the West Indies (Agreement of February 10, 1961; *TIAS* 4734), the Netherlands (Agreement of August 13, 1954; entered into force November 16, 1954; 6 *UST* 103; *TIAS* 3174), and Libya (Agreement of February 24, 1955; applicable from October 30, 1954; 7 *UST* 2051; *TIAS* 3607). The Libya agreement specifies cases in which Libya might be particularly concerned as "an offense against the safety of the Libyan State, an offense against the sovereignty or honor of the Libyan State, or an offense which the Libyan State considers to be of serious public concern, including sexual offenses which cause serious public concern." Even in such cases, however, Libya agrees to give "sympathetic consideration" to a United States request for waiver, *TIAS* 3607, provision d.

that it must request the waiver from the Philippines. In this sense the United States-Philippine agreement stands somewhere between the waiver provisions of the NATO SOFA and the "automatic" waiver provisions of the United States-Japanese status of forces agreement. The latter agreement "requires that when an offense subject to the primary jurisdiction of Japan occurs, if no positive action is taken by Japan to assert jurisdiction, a waiver of the right is deemed to have been made."[20]

In addition to the departure from the NATO SOFA set forth in Agreed Official Minute Number 4, the United States-Philippine agreement also differs in the detailed procedures it requires if a waiver is desired. According to Agreed Implementing Arrangement Number 1, if a waiver of the other government's primary right to exercise jurisdiction is desired, it must be made in the form of a written request "within ten days of receipt of notification of the commission of an offense." Implementing Arrangement Number 1 further provides:

> If either Government is not advised by the other Government within fifteen days of the date of receipt by such other Government of a request for a waiver of jurisdiction that jurisdiction will be exercised by such other Government... the requesting Government shall be free to exercise jurisdiction.

Thus if the United States were to request a waiver of jurisdiction from the Philippines, for example, this positive action by the United States would have to be met by a similar positive action by the Philippine authorities within fifteen days if the latter wished to retain jurisdiction. This provision increases the similarity between the waiver provisions of the United States-Philippine agreement and the United States-Japanese agreement.

Arrangement Number 1 further states:

> If either Government, however, notifies the other Government that for special reasons it desires to reserve decision with respect to the exercise of jurisdiction, the requesting Government will not be free to exercise its jurisdiction until notice is received that the other Government will not exercise jurisdiction or until the expiration of an additional period of fifteen days, whichever is sooner.

Under these requirements, in cases of waiver requests the decision as to which state will exercise jurisdiction must be reached within a maximum of forty days.

Arrangement Number 1 also provides that in order to dispose expeditiously of offenses of "minor importance" the United States military

[20] Baldwin, pp. 83–84, citing Agreed View No. 40, annexed to the Protocol to Amend Article XVII of the Administrative Agreement, September 29, 1953; 4 *UST* 1846; *TIAS* 2848. This provision remains in the agreement of January 19, 1960; 11 *UST* 1652; *TIAS* 4510.

authorities and the competent Philippine authorities may arrange "to dispense with the necessity for a request for a waiver of jurisdiction to be made in each particular case." This presumably was included so as to enable the establishment of some form of blanket waiver of jurisdiction in certain classes of cases without going through the formal procedure of paragraph 3(c), Agreed Official Minute Number 4, and Agreed Implementing Arrangement Number 1. This arrangement and the fact that in waiver cases the proper authorities to consult are the United States commander and the city or provincial fiscal concerned (Agreed Implementing Arrangement Number 1) indicate that the agreement was designed to meet the problem of waivers at the lower levels of decision making.

Base Security

Paragraph 10(a) provides that the United States authorities have the right to police "any camps, establishments or other premises which they occupy as a result of an agreement with the Republic of the Philippines." In so doing the United States military police are given the authority "to take all appropriate measures to ensure the maintenance of order and security of such premises." It is further provided in paragraph 10(b) that United States military police will be used off the bases "only subject to arrangements" with the Philippine authorities "and in liaison with those authorities, and insofar as such employment is necessary to maintain discipline and order among the members of the United States armed forces."

The provisions of paragraphs 10(a) and 10(b) of the Philippine agreement differ from the corresponding provisions of the NATO SOFA with respect to only one word. The NATO SOFA provides that the military police of the sending state may "take all appropriate measures to ensure the maintenance of order and security *on* [emphasis added] such premises," whereas the United States-Philippine agreement provides for the maintenance of order and security *of* such premises. Important differences in interpretation can be given to these two words. "On" as used in the NATO SOFA may be read so as to preclude any action outside the base, whereas "of" in the Philippine agreement may be read so as to permit such action to ensure the order and security of the base.

Whether or not this is a legitimate interpretation, the United States authorities are permitted to take some action outside the base areas, as provided in Agreed Implementing Arrangement Number 2(a). This Arrangement states that the United States military authorities "may apprehend inside and in the vicinity of the United States bases any person in the commission or attempting commission of an offense against the security of that base."[21] This provision further states that if such a person or persons is not subject to United States military law, he "shall immediately be turned over to the Philippine authorities for compliance with formalities required by Philippine law and for custody except as provided by Agreed Minute Number 5."[22] In spite of the latter provision, it would seem that United States action outside the bases may offer numerous opportunities for future conflicts of authority. This is particularly true when it is noted that the provisions of Arrangement Number 2(a) appear to conflict substantially with those of paragraph 10(b), in that the United States military police are allowed to act outside the base by the provisions of the former but not by the provisions of the latter, except through "arrangements with" and "in liaison with" the Philippine authorities, and in that the former seems to provide that the military police may apprehend any offender while the latter mentions only United States military personnel.[23] It seems likely that the intent of Arrangement Number 2(a) is to amplify and clarify paragraphs 10(a) and 10(b). However, it appears to have added confusion rather than clarity and thus has increased the possibility of future conflicts over actions taken by United States personnel "in the vicinity"—whatever that might be taken to mean—of the bases.[24]

Additional provisions pertaining to base security are found in paragraph 11. Under the provisions of this paragraph, the Philippine government is obligated to seek and enforce such legislation as it deems necessary "to ensure the adequate security and protection within its

[21] In spite of the usage of "on" in the corresponding provision of the United States-Japanese agreement, the addition of an Agreed Minute creates the same situation as exists in the Philippine Agreement of 1965. See Agreed Minute for Article XVII, re paragraph 10(a) and 10(b), Agreement of January 19, 1960, *TIAS* 4510.

[22] Agreed Minute No. 5 excludes the turning over for custody of members of the United States civilian component or dependents.

[23] In the Philippine agreement no reference is made from Arrangement No. 2(a) back to a specific paragraph of the Article itself. However, in the Japanese agreement a provision similar to Arrangement 2(a) in the Philippine agreement specifically refers to paragraph 10(a) and 10(b) of Article XVII of the Japanese agreement. See above, note 21.

[24] Although no statement appears in the new Philippine agreement pertaining to the term "vicinity," such a statement is included in the Japanese agreement. In that agreement vicinity is to be interpreted to mean "a place so near to facilities or areas as to make possible the commission or attempted commission of security offenses." Cho, "Jurisdiction over Foreign Forces in Japan, 1945–1960," p. 62, citing Agreed View No. 24, adopted by the Committee on Jurisdiction on July 30, 1952. This interpretation, however, is only slightly more specific than the term it is trying to interpret.

territory of installations, equipment, property, records, and official information of the United States Government..."

Arrest and Confinement

Paragraph 5(a) provides for mutual assistance between the United States authorities and the Philippine authorities in cases involving "the arrest of members of the United States armed forces or civilian component and their dependents and in handing them over" to the proper authority which is to exercise jurisdiction. It is further stated in paragraph 5(b) that the Philippine authorities "shall notify promptly" the United States authorities in the event "of the arrest of any member of the United States armed forces or civilian component or a dependent." Additionally, if a member of the United States armed forces or civilian component or dependent over whom the Philippine authorities are to exercise jurisdiction is in the custody of the United States, paragraph 5(c) provides that he shall remain in such custody "until he is charged by the Republic of the Philippines."

Agreed Minute Number 5, however, qualifies these paragraphs in such a way as to retain the provisions for custody substantially as they have been historically. According to Minute 5 the "custody of an accused member of the United States armed forces, civilian component, or dependent" over which the Philippines is to exercise jurisdiction "shall be entrusted without delay to the commanding officer of the nearest base," pending investigation, trial and final judgment. When the commanding officer receives such a person, he shall acknowledge in writing:

> (a) that such accused has been delivered to him for custody pending investigation, trial and final judgment in a competent court of the Philippines and (b) that he will be made available to the Philippine authorities for investigation upon their request and (c) that he will be produced before said court when required by it.

Upon the filing of the information against the accused in the competent court, the commanding officer will be furnished with a copy by the fiscal. Under such provisions a case similar to the Roe case, where the accused was shipped out of the Philippines before being tried, still may arise. The only means of eliminating such a recurrence is through a more rapid Philippine judicial process and the continued good faith of the United States military authorities in the Philippines.

In addition to the special treatment received by a member of the United States armed forces, civilian component, or a dependent who is taken into custody, special treatment also is received if he is confined by a ruling of a Philippine court. In this connection Agreed Implementing Arrangement Number 3 provides for mutual agreement by the United States and the Philippine authorities on facilities to be used for confinement. It also provides that appropriate United States authorities will be allowed to visit such persons and in appropriate cases provide "supplementary care and provisions for such persons, such as clothing, food, bedding, and medical and dental treatment."

These arrangements are very similar to those of the 1947 agreement, under which the practice relative to confinement was, upon occasion, even more lenient than that formally specified. One such case involved an airman who had been convicted of "frustrated homicide" and confined by a Philippine court to an indeterminant period of from six months and one day to six years and one day. United States procedure in such situations requires the local military authorities to make at least monthly inspection visits. On one such visit it was noted by the inspection personnel that although the airman was receiving better treatment than Filipinos in the same prison, he was losing weight. His food was therefore supplemented by his command. United States Embassy inquiries later led to a recommendation for the conditional release of the airman. This recommendation was referred to and approved by President Garcia.[25] As this case indicates, United States-Philippine cooperation in the area of confinement procedures has been highly satisfactory in the past. There appears to be no reason to expect it to be otherwise in the future.

The provisions of paragraphs 5(a) and 5(b) pertaining to arrests are amplified further by Agreed Arrangement Number 2. This Arrangement provides that "normally" the United States military authorities will "make all arrests, or otherwise take persons into custody, within U.S. bases." However, this provision is not intended to preclude arrests by Philippine authorities "where the base commander or his authorized representative has given consent, or in the case of pursuit of a flagrant offender who has committed a serious crime." This provision departs from the provisions of the 1947 agreement in its inclusion of the "pursuit of a flagrant offender" by the Philippine authorities. As such, it offers distinct possibilities of conflicts of authority, particularly in cases involving a Philippine authority pursuing onto a base a member of the United States armed forces, civilian component, or a dependent. The successful operation of such a provision will require considerable cooper-

[25] See *Operation Hearings 1959*, p. 25.

ation between the base authorities and the local Philippine authorities, a cooperation which has not always existed in the past.

Implementing Arrangement 2 further provides:

> If the Philippine authorities desire that persons not subject to the jurisdiction of the U.S. armed forces who are within U.S. bases be arrested or taken into custody, the U.S. military authorities will undertake, upon request, and within the limits of their authority, to make the arrest or take them into custody.

According to Agreed Official Minute Number 7 the United States will not "grant asylum in any of the bases to any person fleeing from the lawful jurisdiction of the Philippines" and any such person found on any base will be surrendered "on demand" to the competent Philippine authorities.

Search and Seizure

In addition to the cooperation called for in paragraphs 5(a) and 5(b) with respect to arrests, there also are provisions in paragraph 6(a) for mutual assistance in carrying out necessary investigations into offenses and "in the collection and production of evidence including the seizure and, in proper cases, the handing over of objects connected with an offense," provided, however, that the handing over of such objects may "be made subject to their return within the time specified by the authority delivering them." This provision for mutual assistance is supplemented by Agreed Implementing Arrangement 2(b) which appears to be aimed at lessening the possibility of conflict of authority on the bases. This Arrangement specifies that normally the authorities of the Philippines will not exercise

> the right of search, seizure, or inspection with respect to any persons or property within the bases in use by and guarded under the authority of the United States armed forces or with respect to property of the United States armed forces wherever situated, except in cases where the competent authorities of the United States armed forces consent to such search, seizure, or inspection by the Philippine authorities of such persons or property.

In spite of this prohibition of search, seizure, or inspection without the permission of the United States authorities, the United States authorities are obligated under the provisions of Arrangement 2(b) to "undertake, upon request, and within the limits of their authority, to make such a search, seizure, or inspection" when it is desired by the authorities of the Philippines. It is further provided that in the event of a judgment concerning such property, except property owned or utilized by the United States Government or its instrumentalities, the United States, to the extent permitted under its law, will turn over such property to the Philippine authorities for disposition in accordance with the judgment.

Thus paragraph 6(a) specifically provides for mutual assistance and cooperation between the United States and Philippine authorities. Although one might presume that cooperation and mutual assistance in carrying out the provisions of an international agreement would be implicit in the agreement itself, some conflict may be avoided by making such cooperation and assistance a definite treaty commitment.

Procedural Guarantees

Section 9 of the revised Article XIII is the bill of rights section. By its provisions if a member of the United States armed forces or civilian component or a dependent is prosecuted by Philippine authorities, he shall be entitled:

(a) to a prompt and speedy trial;
(b) to be informed, in advance of trial, of the specific charge or charges against him;
(c) to be confronted with the witnesses against him;
(d) to have compulsory process for obtaining witnesses in his favor if they are within the jurisdiction of the Republic of the Philippines;
(e) to have legal representation of his own choice for his defense or to have free or assisted legal representation under the conditions prevailing for the time being in the Republic of the Philippines;[26]
(f) if he considers it necessary, to have the services of a competent interpreter;
(g) to communicate with a representative of the Government of the United States; and
(h) to have a representative of the United States Government present at his trial, which will be public except when the court decrees otherwise in accordance with Philippine law.

This section, which is almost a verbatim copy of the bill of rights section of the NATO SOFA, is a completely new addition to the United

[26] It should also be pointed out in connection with this provision that the United States Congress has authorized the military, through Public Law 777 (70 *Stat.* 630, 1906), to employ counsel and pay fees, court costs, bail, and other expenses incidental to representation, before foreign courts of persons subject to the U.C.M.J. Under this law the military authorities have usually spent from $50,000 to $65,000 per year in defending United States military personnel abroad. This law offers valuable added protection for American military personnel in the Philippines. See *Operation Hearings 1957–Operation Hearings 1965.* As one report stated, the United States military personnel appearing in criminal proceedings are far better off than most Filipinos, primarily because they usually have the services of the better attorneys in the Philippines. Interview with Governor Sering in New Orleans, May 29, 1966.

States-Philippine agreement. With the exception of paragraphs (f), (g), and (h), however, all of the provisions are included in the Philippine Constitution as guaranteed rights for all persons in the Philippines accused of criminal offenses.[27]

The only difficulty with respect to these jurisdictional provisions which has arisen in the past has resulted from the slow judicial process. Since little is being done to speed up this process, it is likely that it will continue to present problems at least for the immediate future.[28]

An additional procedural safeguard for members of the United States armed forces stationed in the Philippines is the prohibition of double jeopardy. Paragraph 8 provides that where one of the parties to the agreement has tried an accused and he

> has been acquitted, or has been convicted and is serving, or has served, his sentence or has been pardoned, he may not be tried again for the same offense within the same territory by the authorities of the other State... [except that this provision shall do nothing to prevent the United States] from trying a member of its force for any violation of rules or discipline arising from an act or omission which constituted an offense for which he was tried by the authorities of the Republic of the Philippines.

Potential Problems

In addition to the problems mentioned above which might arise under the revised Article XIII, there are a number of other potential problems which should be discussed. One such problem arises under the provisions of paragraph 3(b)(i). There is a distinct possibility that of all the provisions in the new agreement, this paragraph is potentially the most controversial. As noted above, the United States has the primary right to exercise jurisdiction over all persons subject to its military law in relation to "(1) offenses... solely against the person or property of a member of the United States armed forces or civilian component or of a dependent." Since the term "civilian component" is not defined in either the 1947 agreement or the new agreement, there is nothing that explicitly excludes Filipino employees of the United States from being regarded as members of the civilian component. Therefore, paragraph 3(b)(i) could be interpreted to mean that the United States has the primary right to exercise jurisdiction over persons subject to its military law for offenses against Filipino civilian employees

[27] See Article III, paragraph 17 of the Constitution of the Philippines.

[28] According to one report the major reason for this problem is simply the fact that there are too few judges and too many cases. Interview with Governor Sering in New Orleans, May 29, 1966. As had already been noted, however, the judicial procedure used in the Philippines is also a major contributing factor.

of the United States. Such an interpretation is not possible in the case of either the NATO SOFA or the United States-Japanese agreement because they contain definitions which explicitly exclude nationals of the host state from the term "civilian component."[29]

The reason or reasons for this omission in the United States-Philippine agreement are not known. There are, however, three possible explanations. First, the question of the absence of a definition and the possible ramifications of this absence may simply have been overlooked. This is unlikely. Second, there may be no dispute over the definition, and it may have been omitted with the understanding that the definition was identical with that put forth in the NATO and Japanese agreements, after which the Philippine agreement is patterned. Third, a definition may have been excluded intentionally because of disagreement over its content. As has been noted in Chapter V, one of the reasons for the reluctance of the United States to amend the original Article XIII was that the bases in the Philippines employ thousands of Filipinos and that there existed the possibility of "a demoralization of base personnel if the Filipinos could invoke their own criminal laws against officers and enlisted men."[30] Should the United States still hold to this view, it may be that Ambassador Blair refused to agree to a definition of civilian component which explicitly excluded Filipino employees. If this is the case, serious difficulties may arise under this provision of the new agreement.

It should be pointed out, however, that even if the United States were to obtain an interpretation of paragraph 3(b)(i) whereby it would have primary jurisdiction over those subject to United States military law for offenses committed against Filipinos, it would in no case under the new agreement have the right to exercise jurisdiction over Philippine nationals or persons "ordinarily resident" in the Philippines, "unless they are members of the United States armed forces." The latter provision, as noted above, was included in paragraph 4 and makes it perfectly clear that even if the United States law with respect to the trial of members of the civilian component is reversed, the United States would not be able to exercise jurisdiction over Filipinos. At the same time, however, parargraph 4 may create serious problems relative to the security guards on United States bases. Under its provisions Philippine authorities clearly have exclusive jurisdiction over alleged

[29] For Japan, see Agreement of January 19, 1960, *TIAS* 4510, Article I, paragraph b. For the NATO countries, see Article I, paragraph 1(b), Agreement of June 19, 1951, *TIAS* 2846.

[30] *New York Times*, September 4, 1956, p. 10.

criminal offenses committed by Filipino guards on the bases. Recent correspondence with the Director of International Law at Clark Field reveals that at present "approximately 11 cases [are] pending against our security and Negrito guards for their action in protecting government property and personnel."[31] If in the future a situation develops in which the security guards are unable to perform their duties for fear of prosecution in Philippine courts, United States-Philippine relations might be seriously impaired.

Difficulties also may arise with respect to United States military security guards. As has been noted, paragraph 3(b)(ii) grants the United States the right to exercise primary jurisdiction over persons subject to its military law in cases involving "offenses arising out of any act or omission done in the performance of official duty."

In spite of the attempts in Agreed Minutes Number 2 and Number 3 to clarify the term "official duty" much room for conflict remains. Jurisdiction over a case such as the Cole case or any other case in which United States personnel are not "on duty" now clearly would come within the primary jurisdiction of the Philippines. There is, however, a twilight zone in which conflicts over jurisdiction can easily arise when cases involve instances of indiscretion on the part of United States personnel on "official duty." Such a case, involving the killing of a civilian by Specialist Third Class William S. Girard, arose under the United States-Japanese agreement. Stambuk summarizes the facts of the case as follows:

> The incident occurred on a part-time firing range during a break in military exercises when Girard and another soldier were left in the area to guard military equipment which remained there while the units engaged changed their positions. The woman was one of a group of Japanese civilians who came to the firing range to gather scrap brass—a regular practice generally tolerated by American officers, except that there was concern about keeping the scavengers out of the line of fire... The two soldiers left on duty during the break allegedly first threw some expended cartridges toward the scavengers, inviting them to come closer for more. When some of them approached, Girard fired two expended cartridges from the grenade launcher attached to his rifle, and hit a fleeing woman in the back [causing her death]. [Girard's] commanding officer issued a certificate stating that the shot was fired as a warning while Girard was on duty, and that the United States intended to exercise jurisdiction in the case.[32]

Under the United States-Japanese agreement such a certificate is considered to be conclusive in all judicial proceedings "unless the contrary is proved."[33] Under Agreed View Number 43, however, if the Chief

[31] Personal letter from Captain Hackett, dated June 15, 1966.

[32] Stambuk, p. 89. See also the excellent study of the *Girard* case by Baldwin, pp. 52–106.

[33] Applicable at the time was paragraph 3(a) (ii), Agreement of September 29, 1953,

Prosecutor of Japan considers that there is proof to the contrary, and if the commanding officer refuses to accept this proof, the matter is turned over to the United States-Japan Joint Committee for decision.[34] This is what occurred in the Girard case. However, the Joint Committee, composed of one Japanese and one American, was unable to reach an agreement until finally, after four months of discussion, the United States agreed to waive the right to exercise jurisdiction. Before being disposed of, the Girard case created a substantial disturbance in Japan, certainly as much as either the Roe case or the Cole case did in the Philippines.[35]

In view of the past incidents involving security guards which have occurred at Clark Field and Subic Bay it is highly possible that cases similar to the Girard case will occur in the Philippines. Although the revised United States-Philippine agreement attempts to clarify the term "official duty," it is likely that questions about its interpretation will still arise. As Baldwin has pointed out, "no single concept has yet been formulated to determine duty status within the meaning of the jurisdictional provisions of status of force agreements."[36]

Problems concerning the waiver of the primary right to exercise jurisdiction might arise due to an omission in paragraph 3(c). There is no indication in this paragraph whether a state which has waived its primary right may nevertheless exercise jurisdiction should the other state fail to proceed to trial. This type of situation was illustrated in the French case of *Aitchison* c. *Whitley*, involving a member of the Canadian Air Force and a member of the United States Air Force.[37] In this case

TIAS 2848. The same provision is included at Agreed Minute for Article XVII, re paragraph 3(a) (ii), in the Agreement of January 19, 1960, *TIAS* 4510.

[34] See Baldwin, pp. 62–63, citing Agreed View No. 43 of the Subcommittee on Jurisdiction, Administrative Agreement Matters, Far Eastern Command, Pamphlet 27–1 (January 1956).

[35] In the United States the *Girard* case revived the isolationist attack against the status of forces agreements and became the occasion for a special session of the Senate Committee on Armed Services. See U.S., Congress, Senate, Committee on Armed Services, *Hearings, On the Case of United States Army Specialist Third Class William S. Girard...*, 85th Cong., 1st Sess., 1957. In addition it became the subject of a constitutional test as to whether a member of the United States military could be turned over to foreign authorities by the United States military authorities under a status of forces agreement. The right to do so was upheld by the Supreme Court. *Wilson* v. *Girard*, 354 U.S. 524 (1957).

[36] Baldwin, p. 82. For general discussions of the possible criteria for determining the meaning of official duty, see *ibid.*, pp. 52–106 *passim*; Snee and Pye, pp. 46–54, and Appendix III, pp. 144–167; and Stambuk, pp. 84–96.

[37] *Aitchison* c. *Whitley*, Tribunal correctionel de Corbeil, 5 avril 1954, *43 Revue critique de droit international privé* 602–612 (1954), *,Annuaire français de droit international* 579 (1955); *Whitley* c. *Aitchison*, Cours d'appeal de Paris, 16 mai 1956, 46 *Revue critique...* 100 (1957), 3 *Annuaire...* 721 (1957); reversed, Cours de Cassation, Chambre Criminelle, 1958, 43 *Revue generale de droit international public*, 17–18 (1959); and *Operation Hearings 1958*, p. 43. The best analysis of the *Whitley* case is found in Stambuk, pp. 96–106. See also Snee and Pye, pp. 63–

the defendant, Whitley, was off duty when the offense occurred and therefore was subject to the primary jurisdiction of France. The United States authorities, however, asked for and received a waiver. An informal air force investigation was carried out, and Whitley was absolved of responsibility. Therefore, no court-martial occurred, and France was so notified. Soon afterwards a civil suit for damages, combined with a criminal prosecution, was brought against Whitley.[38] He was convicted in the lower French court and was fined. The Court of Cassation later reversed the lower court's judgment, but the case was not heard until after Whitley's insurance company had settled the claim. As Stambuk has noted, the latter point makes it difficult to set forth the ruling of the high court as an ironbound precedent even in France.[39]

Certainly the possibility exists that a similar problem with respect to waiver provisions might arise in the Philippines. As Rouse and Baldwin have stated, in order to accomplish the purpose of the status of forces agreements, conflicts of jurisdiction should be resolved "quickly and with finality."[40] The United States-Philippine agreement might have come closer to resolving this particular conflict if it had included a provision similar to the provision in the United States-Libyan agreement which states that a waiver in a case "shall be final and thereafter the Libyan authorities will not exercise jurisdiction in relation to such a case."[41] An addition of this nature to Minute Number 4 would have clarified paragraph 3(c) and decreased the possibility of conflict over the waiver procedure.

Under the provisions of the revised agreement the problem of jurisdictional lacunae still exists. It is possible for cases to arise similar to the Brownell case and the *Hirshberg* case, which were discussed in Chapter I, and the Roe case, which was discussed in Chapter IV.[42] If an offense involving a member of the United States armed forces were to occur in the Philippines and the offender were to be discharged prior to trial, United States military authorities would be unable to exercise jurisdiction under existing United States constitutional practice.[43] Because

72; and Edwin G. Schuck, "Concurrent Jurisdiction Under the NATO Status of Forces Agreement," 57 *Columbia Law Review* 355, 355–371 (1957).

[38] In France as in the Philippines the civil and criminal aspects of a case may be combined.

[39] Stambuk, pp. 105–106.

[40] Rouse and Baldwin, p. 49.

[41] Provision d, Memorandum of Understanding Relating to Jurisdiction over United States Armed Forces under the Agreement of September 9, 1954 [5 *UST* 2449; *TIAS* 3107]. Signed at Tripoli February 24, 1955; entered into force February 24, 1955; applicable from October 30, 1954. 7 *UST* 2051; *TIAS* 3607.

[42] See above, pp. 4–5, 13, 55–59.

[43] See above, chap. I, note 49.

of the absence of an extradition treaty between the United States and the Philippines, Philippine authorities would be unable to exercise jurisdiction in a case in which the accused had been discharged and shipped back to the United States before being tried. This is true in spite of the provisions of the 1965 agreement which gave the Philippines the right to exercise jurisdiction over all crimes committed by United States personnel in the Philippines.

Conclusion

When viewed in its entirety, the revised jurisdictional arrangement between the United States and the Philippines appears to be a significant improvement over the original Article XIII. As such it should lead to a decrease in the irritants that have plagued United States-Philippine relations over the years. As has been noted, however, there are numerous aspect of the agreement which may lead to future jurisdictional conflicts. In addition, jurisdictional lacunae still exist.

Many of the problems which may arise under the 1965 agreement are similar to those which have arisen under other status of forces agreements but there are some which are present in the United States-Philippine agreement which are not typical. Several of these have arisen out of the attempt to adopt the criminal jurisdictional provisions of the NATO SOFA as Article XIII and to supplement this article with Agreed Official Minutes and Agreed Implementing Arrangements. This procedure sometimes has led to confusion rather than clarification. Other potential areas of difficulty have been produced by representing the provisions of the 1965 agreement to the Philippine public as copies of the NATO SOFA provisions. Public disillusionment well might occur if, for example, a security guard while in the performance of official duty were to kill a Filipino off base but "in the vicinity of" the base, and under the revised agreement the United States were to claim primary jurisdiction. Such an unfortunate incident could give rise to serious public relations problems for the United States, particularly since the Philippines has a highly vocal and unhampered press.

CHAPTER VII

TOWARD A CONJURISDICTIONAL LAW

In their study of the NATO Status of Forces Agreement (SOFA), Snee and Pye stated that a new conjurisdictional law was being developed with respect to the right to exercise criminal jurisdiction under status of forces agreements. Their study and most other studies, however, are concerned only with the jurisdictional arrangements under the NATO agreement. If a new law is developing, it will evolve not only from the NATO agreement but also from other less publicized agreements. Therefore, these other agreements must be studied in order to determine if the NATO SOFA is setting a standard for the development of such a law.

The present study has been concerned with the United States-Philippine agreement. It has shown that historically the United States-Philippine criminal jurisdictional arrangements were significantly different from those of the NATO SOFA. Two important factors which contributed to this difference were the former status of the Philippines as a colony of the United States and the fact that the Philippines was an underdeveloped state.

During the approximately fifty years the two countries were bound by the ties of colonialism two peace time jurisdictional patterns existed, one civil oriented and the other military oriented. Of the two, the military-oriented pattern was dominant in the Philippines immediately prior to and immediately after World War II. In many respects this military-oriented pattern was carried over into the independence period in the form of the Military Bases Agreement of 1947.

According to the provisions of this agreement, the United States had the right to exercise jurisdiction over all criminal offenses committed off the bases in which only members of the United States armed forces were involved and in all cases in which the offense arose out of an act or omission done in the performance of official duty. These provisions were basically the same as those later included in the NATO SOFA. In the Philippines, however, the United States additionally had the right to exercise jurisdiction over all criminal offenses committed on the bases except those involving only Filipinos and those involving Philippine national security. The United States, therefore, had the right to exercise jurisdiction over all cases on the bases in which an American committed an offense against a Filipino. Thus, under the original United States-Philippine agreement the United States had much wider jurisdictional competence over its own personnel than it later had under the NATO SOFA. Moreover, under the same provisions the United States had the right to exercise jurisdiction over Filipinos for offenses committed on the bases, provided the offense was not against another Filipino. The right to exercise such jurisdiction over a national of the receiving state was specifically precluded by the provisions of the NATO SOFA.

The second factor which caused the United States-Philippine agreement to differ from the NATO agreement, the status of the Philippines as an underdeveloped state, not only led to United States demands for wider jurisdictional rights but also contributed to numerous problems in implementing the 1947 agreement, problems which were not so prevalent in implementing the NATO SOFA. For example, the sharp contrast between the standard of living of the base personnel and the local Philippine population seemed to be responsible at least partially for base security problems that are not present to the same degree in the NATO countries. Problems such as this would seem to indicate that the implementation of a status of forces agreement in one environment may involve difficulties which are not present in another environment. Therefore, it may be appropriate for status of forces agreements with underdeveloped states to include provisions which are different from those of the NATO SOFA.

At the same time, however, there may be another factor involved in the stationing of the troops of a developed state in an underdeveloped state which mitigates the importance of the environmental factor. This is the concern of the underdeveloped state with the questions of sovereignty and equality. Although the presence of foreign troops in any country might act as a stimulus to nationalism, this seems to be true particularly with respect to new, underdeveloped states such as the Philippines. Thus while the environment of the receiving state might call for criminal jurisdictional provisions which are different from the provisions of the NATO SOFA, the force of nationalism in the underdeveloped state might call for equality with the NATO countries. This appears to be the development which occurred in the Philippines, where demands for revision of the 1947 agreement may be looked upon as an attempt by the Philippines to legalize its sovereignty and equality via international law.

The agreement of August 10, 1965, which includes the revised Article XIII, the Agreed Official Minutes, and the Agreed Implementing Arrangements, appears to have solved numerous problems which were present under the original agreement. Although, as has been pointed out, there are problems which the revised agreement has not solved and problems which it may have created, the revised Article XIII itself is almost identical to the corresponding provisions of the NATO SOFA. Therefore, the 1965 agreement appears basically to have satisfied, at least with respect to the jurisdictional arrangements, the desire of the Philippines for full acceptance as an independent nation.

The present study, as a study of a status of forces agreement involving an underdeveloped state, has pointed out problems which are not present under the NATO agreement or the United States-Japanese agreement.[1] In spite of this, as has been shown, the Philippines demanded criminal jurisdictional arrangements on a par with those of the parties to the NATO SOFA and on a par with those in the United States-Japanese agreement. Such demands are not in agreement with studies which have emphasized that the new nations are seeking a "new" international law.[2] With respect to status of forces agreements at least, it seems that what is being demanded is not a new international law but rather an international law which treats the new states on an equal basis with the older, established states. Although qualifications imposed by added Minutes and Arrangements cause the United States-

[1] Presumably this would also apply in the case of the recently concluded United States-Australian agreement. The criminal jurisdictional arrangements under this agreement are the same as those in the NATO SOFA, with no added "minutes" or "understandings" such as one finds in the United States-Philippine agreement or the United States-Japanese agreement. See Article 8, Status of United States Forces in Australia, signed at Canberra May 9, 1963, entered into force May 9, 1963; *TIAS* 5349.

[2] See, for example, Josef L. Kunz, "Pluralism of Legal and Value Systems and International Law," 49 *AJIL* 370–376 (1955); Kunz, "The Changing Law of Nations," 51 *AJIL* 77–83 (1957); Statement of Luis Padilla, 1 *Yearbook of the International Law Commission* 155–156 (1957); Jorge Castaneda, "The Underdeveloped Nations and the Development of International Law," 15 *International Organization* 38–48 (1961); R. P. Anand, "Role of the 'New' Asian-African Countries in the Present International Legal Order," 56 *AJIL* 383–406 (1962); Edward McWhinney, "The 'New' Countries and the 'New' International Law: The United Nations' Special Conference on Friendly Relations and Co-Operation Among States," 60 *AJIL* 1–33 (1966); and J. J. G. Syatauw, *Some Newly Established Asian States and the Development of International Law* (The Hague: Martinus Nijhoff, 1961).

Philippine agreement to fall somewhat short of that goal,[3] Article XIII itself, as has been indicated, is almost a verbatim copy of the NATO provisions. The case of the United States-Philippine agreement thus seems to provide strong evidence that the NATO SOFA is performing a general *de lege ferenda* function by projecting the standard for an international norm relative to the right to exercise criminal jurisdiction over members of a visiting force.[4] If this is true, other lesser states might very well follow the lead of the Philippines in demanding a revision of their status of forces agreements.[5] Should this occur, it is hoped that the present study will suggest some of the potential problems involved and their possible solutions.

It is hoped also that this study will assist in pointing out and hence help eliminate future difficulties relative to the United States bases in the Philippines. Given the deep involvement of the United States in Southeast Asia and the importance of the United States bases in the Philippines, it is particularly important at the present time that the two states maintain good relations. Should this study assist in furthering the "special relationship" that has existed between the United States and the Philippines, the author will be gratified.

[3] It should be pointed out, however, that in some instances, most notably with respect to waiver provisions, supplemental bilateral agreements between the United States and other NATO countries approach the provisions of the United States-Philippine agreement. See, for example, Annex to Stationing of United States Armed Forces in the Netherlands, signed at The Hague August 13, 1954, entered into force November 16, 1954, 6 *UST* 103, *TIAS* 3174; and Article II, paragraph 1, Agreement Between the United States of America and the Kingdom of Greece Covering the Status of United States Forces in Greece, signed at Athens September 7, 1956, entered into force September 7, 1956, 7 *UST* 2555, *TIAS* 3649.

[4] Additional evidence is supplied by the agreement between the United States and Korea, which was published while the present study was in the final stages of preparation. Under this agreement the right to exercise jurisdiction over United States forces is basically the same as under the United States-Philippine agreement. See Article XXII, Facilities and Areas and the Status of United States Armed Forces in Korea, with Agreed Minutes, Agreed Understandings and Exchange of Letters, signed at Seoul July 9, 1966, entered into force May 9, 1967, *TIAS* 6127.

[5] Of the published United States agreements, see for example: Agreement... Covering the Defense of Greenland, signed at Copenhagen April 27, 1951, entered into force April 27, 1951, 2 *UST* 1485, *TIAS* 2292; Agreement Concerning the Utilization of Defense Installations in Ethiopia, signed at Washington June 22, 1953, entered into force June 22, 1953, 5 *UST* 749, *TIAS* 2964; Agreement Concerning the Establishment of a Loran Transmitting Station [in the Dominican Republic], signed at Washington March 19, 1957, entered into force March 19, 1957, *TIAS* 3780; Agreement for the Establishment of a Loran Transmitting Station [in Nicaragua], signed at Managua September 5, 1958, entered into force September 5, 1958, 9 *UST* 1206, *TIAS* 4106; Agreement Relating to the Use of Facilities and Services at Dhahran Airfield [Saudi Arabia], signed at Jidda June 18, 1951, entered into force June 18, 1951, 2 *UST* 1466, *TIAS* 2290, extended April 2, 1957, 8 *UST* 403, *TIAS* 3790; and Agreement between the United States of America and the Republic of Korea, signed at Taejan July 12, 1950, entered into force July 12, 1950, 5 *UST* 1408, *TIAS* 3012.

LIST OF CASES CITED

Aitchison c. *Whitley*. Tribunal correctionel de Corbeil, 5 avril 1954, 43 *Revue critique de droit international privé* 602–612 (1954), 1 *Annuaire français de droit international* 579 (1955). Upheld at *Whitley* c. *Aitchison*. Cours d'appel de Paris, 16 mai 1956, 46 *Revue critique*... 100 (1957), 3 *Annuaire français*... 721 (1957). Reversed at Cours de Cassation, Chambre Criminelle, 1958, 43 *Revue générale de droit international public* 17–18 (1959).
Alcantara v. *Director of Prisons*. 75 Phil. 494 (1945).
Asican v. *Quirino*. 75 Phil. 791 (1946).
Co Kim Cham v. *Tan Keh*. 75 Phil. 371 (1945).
Coleman v. *Tennessee*. 97 U.S. 509 (1878).
De La Paz v. *CDR*. 52 *Official Gazette* 3307 (1956).
Dizon v. *Commanding General*. 81 Phil. 286 (1948).
Dow v. *Johnson*. 100 U.S. 158 (1879).
Estate of McDonough v. *Philippine National Bank*. 88 Phil. 625 (1951).
Factor v. *Laubenheimer*. 290 U.S. 276 (1933).
Franklin v. *United States*. 216 U.S. 559 (1910).
Grafton v. *United States*. 206 U.S. 333 (1907).
Grisham v. *Hagen*. 361 U.S. 278 (1960).
Haw Pia v. *China Banking Corporation*. 80 Phil. 604 (1948).
Herrero v. *Dias*. 75 Phil. 489 (1945).
Hirshberg v. *Cooke*. 336 U.S. 210 (1949).
In re Calloway. 1 Phil. 11 (1901).
In re Di Bartalo. 50 F. Supp. 929 (1943).
In re Lo Dolce. 106 F. Supp. 455 (1953).
Kinsella v. *United States ex rel. Singleton*. 361 U.S. 234 (1960).
Kinsella v. *Kruger*. 354 U.S. 1 (1957). Reversing on rehearing, *Kinsella* v. *Kruger*. 351 U.S. 470 (1956).
Liwanag v. *Hamill*. 52 *Official Gazette* 1396 (1956).
Miquiabas v. *Commanding General*. 80 Phil. 262 (1948).
McElroy v. *United States ex rel. Guagliardo*. 361 U.S. 281 (1960).
Pastrana v. *Director of Prisons*. 84 Phil. 357 (1949).
Payomo v. *Floyd*. 42 Phil. 788 (1922).
People v. *Acierto*. 49 *Official Gazette* 518; 92 Phil. 534 (1953).
People v. *Jose*. 75 Phil. 612 (1945).
People v. *Tuason*. 84 Phil. 670 (1949).
Peralta v. *Director of Prisons*. 75 Phil. 285 (1945).
Perlstein v. *United States*. 151 F. 2d 167 (1945). Certiorari dismissed, 328 U.S. 822 (1946).
Raquiza v. *Bradford*. 75 Phil. 50 (1945).
Reid v. *Covert*. 354 U.S. 1 (1957). Reversing on rehearing, *Reid* v. *Covert*. 351 U.S. 487 (1956).

BIBLIOGRAPHY

BOOKS

Aruego, Jose M. *The Framing of the Philippine Constitution*. 2 vols. Manila: University Publishing Co., Inc., 1949.

Bishop, William W., Jr. *International Law*. 2d ed. revised. Boston: Little, Brown and Co., 1962.

Blair, Emma Helen, and Robertson, James Alexander (eds.). *The Philippine Islands 1493–1803*, beginning with Vol. 6 *The Philippine Islands 1493–1898*. 55 vols. Cleveland, Ohio: A. H. Clark Co., 1903–1909.

Blount, James Henderson. *The American Occupation of the Philippines*. New York: G. P. Putnam's Sons, 1912.

Bordwell, Percy. *The Law of War Between Belligerents*. Chicago: Callaghan and Co., 1908.

Davis, George B. *The Elements of International Law*. New York: Harper and Brothers Publishers, 1900.

Deener, David R. *The United States Attorneys General and International Law*. The Hague: Martinus Nijhoff, 1957.

Ebb, Lawrence F. *International Business*. St. Paul, Minn.: West Publishing Co., 1964.

Elliott, Charles B. *The Philippines to the End of the Military Regime*. Indianapolis: Bobbs-Merrill Co., 1916.

Fenwick, Charles G. *International Law*. 2d ed. revised. New York: D. Appleton-Century Co., 1934.

Fernandez, Leandro H. *The Philippine Republic*. New York: Columbia University, 1926.

Forbes, William Cameron. *The Philippine Islands*. 2 vols. Boston: Houghton Mifflin Co., 1928.

Foreman, John. *The Philippine Islands*. New York: Charles Scribner's Sons, 1899.

Grunder, Garel A., and Livezey, William E. *The Philippines and the United States*. Norman: University of Oklahoma Press, 1951.

Hayden, Joseph Ralston. *The Philippines*. New York: Macmillan Co., 1942.

Henderson, James M. *Republic of the Philippines Digest*. 8 vols. Manila: Lawyers Co-Operative Publishing Co., 1960.

Kalaw, Maximo M. *Self-Government in the Philippines*. New York: Century Co., 1919.

LeRoy, J. A. *The Americans in the Philippines*. 2 vols. Boston: Houghton, Mifflin Co., 1914.

Magoon, Charles E. *Reports on the Law of Civil Government in Territory Subject to Military Occupation by the Military Forces of the United States*. 2d ed. revised. Washington: Government Printing Office, 1902.

Malcolm, George A. *First Malayan Republic*. Boston: Christopher House, 1951.

Mariño, Salvador L. (Secretary of Justice). *Report to President Macapagal on the U.S. Bases Incidents*. Dated January 30, 1965. Manila: Ilagan and Sanga Press, n.d. Reprinted in 3 *Philippine International Law Journal* 535–550 (1964).

Mayers, Louis. *The American Legal System*. Revised ed. New York: Harper and Brothers, 1964.

Moore, John Bassett. *A Digest of International Law*. 8 vols. Washington: Government Printing Office, 1906.

Muni, Donald S. (ed.) *Philippine Annotated Laws*. 20 vols. Manila: Lawyers Co-Operative Publishing Co., 1956–1958.

Navarro, Emiliano. *A Treatise on the Law of Criminal Procedure in the Philippines*. Manila: Diliman Publishing Co., 1952.

Padilla, Ambrosio. *Criminal Law: Revised Penal Code Annotated*. 2 vols. 8th ed. revised. Manila: Padilla Publications, 1959.

Pascual, Ricardo R., and Majul, Cesar A. *Foreign Policy of the Republic of the Philippines*. New York: Institute of Pacific Relations, 1957.

Progress Magazine 1956. Manila: Manila Times Publishing Co., 1956.

Quezon, Manuel. *The Good Fight*. New York: D. Appleton-Century, 1946.

Ravenholt, Albert. *The Philippines*. Princeton, N.J.: D. Van Nostrand, 1962.

Recto, Claro M. *The Law of Belligerent Occupation with Particular Reference to the Japanese Occupation of the Philippines and the Effect of the Change of Sovereignty on the Commonwealth Treason Law*. Manila: People's Publishers, 1946.

—. *Three Years of Enemy Occupation*. Manila: People's Publishers, 1946.

Reyes, Luis B. *The Revised Penal Code*. 2 vols. 2d ed. revised. Manila: Philaw Publishing, 1956.

Romulo, Carlos P. *Crusade in Asia*. New York: John Day Co., 1955.

Salcedo, Angel S., Reyes, Manuel V., and Gloria, Claro C. *The Armed Forces and the Law*. Quezon City: Capitol Publishing House, Inc., 1958.

Sherwood, Robert E. *Roosevelt and Hopkins*. Revised ed. New York: The University Libiary, 1950.

Smith, Robert Aura. *Philippine Freedom 1946–1958*. New York: Columbia University Press, 1958.

Smith, Roger M., and Somers, Mary F. *Two Papers on Philippine Foreign Policy*. Data Paper No. 38, Southeast Asia Program, Cornell University. Ithaca, New York, January 1960.

Snee, Joseph M., and Pye, Kenneth A. *Status of Forces Agreement*. New York: Oceana Publications, 1957.

Stambuk, George. *American Military Forces Abroad*. Columbus, Ohio: Ohio State University Press, 1963.

Stockton, Charles H. *Outlines of International Law*. New York: Charles Scribner's Sons, 1914.

Syatauw, J. J. G. *Some Newly Established Asian States and the Development of International Law*. The Hague: Martinus Nijhoff, 1961.

Tañada, Lorenzo M., and Fernando, Enrique. *Constitution of the Philippines*. Manila: Citizens Publishing Co., 1953.

Taylor, George E. *The Philippines and the United States*. New York: Frederick A. Praeger, 1964.

Truman, Harry S. *Years of Decision*. Vol. 1 of *Memoirs by Harry S. Truman*. Garden City, N.Y.: Doubleday and Co., Inc., 1955.

Von Glahn, Gerhard. *The Occupation of Enemy Territory*. Minneapolis: University of Minnesota Press, 1957.

Worcester, Dean C., with biographical sketch and four additional chapters by Hayden, Joseph Ralston. *The Philippines Past and Present*. New ed. New York: Macmillan Co., 1930.

ARTICLES AND PERIODICALS

Abrams, Bert A. "International Law and Friendly Foreign Forces," 32 *New York University Law Review* 351–376 (1957).

"Agreements Concerning Military Bases," 3 *Philippine International Law Journal* 438–445 (1964).

Anand, R. P. "Role of the 'New' Asian-African Countries in the Present International Legal Order," 56 *American Journal of International Law* 383–406 (1962).

Badong, Pablo B. "Philippine Jurisdiction Over the George E. Roe Case," 32 *Philippine Law Journal* 403–410 (1957).

Baldwin, Gordon B. "Foreign Jurisdiction and the American Soldier: The Adventures of Girard," 1958 *Wisconsin Law Review* 52–106 (1958).

Barrera, Jesus G. "The Constitution and the Military Bases Agreement," 1957 *Decision Law Journal* 643–655 (1957).

Barton, G. P. "Foreign Armed Forces: Immunity from Criminal Jurisdiction," 27 *British Yearbook of International Law* 186–234 (1950).

—, "Foreign Armed Forces: Immunity from Supervisory Jurisdiction," 26 *British Yearbook of International Law* 380–413 (1949).

—, "Foreign Armed Forces: Qualified Jurisdictional Immunity," 31 *British Yearbook of International Law* 341–370 (1954).

Baxter, R. R. "Criminal Jurisdiction in the NATO Status of Forces Agreement," 7 *International and Comparative Law Quarterly* 72–81 (1958).

Castañeda, Jorge. "The Underdeveloped Nations and the Development of International Law," 15 *International Organization* 38–48 (1961).

Cruz, Emilio Aguillar. "1956... Year of Nationalism," in *Progress Magazine 1956* (Manila: Manila Times Publishing Co., 1956), pp. 18–25.

De Castro, Crispino. "U.S. Jurisdiction Over Armed Forces in the Philippines," 7 *Far Eastern Law Review* 626–651 (1959).

Duke, Robert D., and Vogel, Howard S. "The Constitution and the Standing Army: Another Problem of Court-Martial Jurisdiction," 13 *Vanderbilt Law Review* 435–460 (1960).

Everett, Robert O. "Article 134, Uniform Code of Military Justice—A Study in Vagueness," 37 *North Carolina Law Review* 142–161 (1958).

Glienke, Howard G. "Irritants in P.I.-U.S. Relations," 3 *Kapisanang Pankasaysayan ng Pelipina* [*Historical Bulletin*] 60–95 (1959).

Healy, Gerald W. "The Question of Jurisdiction: American Military Personnel in the Philippines," 3 *Philippine Studies* 287–298 (1957).

Hilario-Soriano, Rafaelita. "U.S.-P.I. Relations," in *Progress Magazine 1956* (Manila: Manila Times Publishing Co., 1956), pp. 42–47, 216–218.

King, Archibald. "Further Developments Concerning Jurisdiction Over Friendly Forces," 40 *American Journal of International Law* 266–279 (1946).

—. "Jurisdiction over Friendly Foreign Armed Forces," 36 *American Journal of International Law* 539–567 (1942).

Kunz, Josef L. "The Changing Law of Nations," 51 *American Journal of International Law* 77–83 (1957).

—. "Pluralism of Legal and Value Systems and International Law," 49 *American Journal of International Law* 370–376 (1955).

Levie, Howard S. "NATO Status of Forces Agreement: Legal Safeguard for American Servicemen," 44 *American Bar Association Journal* 322–326 (1958).

—. "Some Legal Problems Arising Under the NATO Status of Forces Agreement and the Administrative Agreement with Japan," 17 *Federal Bar Journal* 620–625 (1957).

Lockwood, L. D. "The Philippine Supreme Court and Postwar Problems of International Law," 3 *Stanford Law Review* 3–34 (1950).

Manila Times. 1951–1965.

McKay, William P. "The Serviceman and the Law: Personal Liability for Acts and Omissions While Acting in Performance of Official Duties," 42 *University of Detroit Law Journal* 167–194 (1964).

McWhinney, Edward. "The 'New' Countries and the 'New' International Law: The United Nation's Special Conference on Friendly Relations and Co-Operation among States," 60 *American Journal of International Law* 1–33 (1966).

Meron, Theodor. "Some Reflections on the Status of Forces Agreements in the Light of Customary International Law," 6 *International and Comparative Law Quarterly* 689–694 (1957).

"The Military Bases Renegotiations Talks," 2 *Department of Foreign Affairs Review* 53 (1956).

Mill, Edward W. "The New Republic of the Philippines," 15 *Department of State Bulletin*, 475–479 (1946).

—. "The Philippines Prepares for Independence," 14 *Department of State Bulletin* 980–983, 1014 (1946).

Moorhead, Thomas B. "*Reid* v. *Covert* and Its Progeny: The Practical Problem of Punishment," 12 *Syracuse Law Review* 18–25 (1960).

New York Times. 1946–1966.

Note. "Criminal Jurisdiction Over American Armed Forces Abroad," 70 *Harvard Law Review* 1043–1067 (1957).

Orfield, Lester B. "Jurisdiction of Foreign Courts Over Crimes Committed Abroad by American Military Personnel," 8 *South Carolina Law Quarterly* 346–354 (1956).

Osmeña, Sergio. "Philippine Independence and U.S. Amity," 2 *Department of Foreign Affairs Review* 20–23 (1956).

Osmeña, Sergio, Jr. "Speech Delivered at the Luncheon Meeting of the Rotary Club at Manila on September 20, 1956, at the Manila Hotel." Reprinted in 103 *Congressional Record* A207–A209 (1957).

Pacis, Vicente Albano. "Politics of Our Times," in *Progress Magazine 1956* (Manila: Manila Times Publishing Co., 1956), pp. 26–41.

Pascual, R. R., and Majul, C. A. "The Foreign Policy of the Republic [of the Philippines]," 23 *Philippine Social Sciences and Humanities Review* 159–188 (1958).

Pelaez, Emmanuel. "A Hard Look at PI-US Defense Arrangements," 6 *Far Eastern Law Review* 423–433 (1959).

—. "Philippine Foreign Policy: The Whole and Its Parts," 6 *Philippine Journal of Public Administration* 44–50 (1961).

Philippines Free Press. 1946–1965.

Re, Edward D. "The NATO Status of Forces Agreement and International Law," 50 *Northwestern University Law Review* 349–394 (1955).

Reis, John C., and Nibley, Owen S. "Justice, Juries, and Military Dependents," 15 *Western Political Quarterly* 438–448 (1962).

Reyes, Vincente G. "A Note on Jurisdiction Over Friendly Foreign Armed Forces," 3 *Philippine International Law Journal* 133–150 (1964).

Rouse, Joseph H., and Baldwin, Gordon B. "The Exercise of Criminal Jurisdiction Under the NATO Status of Forces Agreement, " 51 *American Journal of International Law* 29–62 (1957).

Schuck, Edwin G. "Concurrent Jurisdiction Under the NATO Status of Forces Agreement," 57 *Columbia Law Review* 355–371 (1957).

Schwartz, Murray L. "International Law and the NATO Status of Forces Agreement," 53 *Columbia Law Review* 1091–1113 (1953).

Schwenk, Edward H. "Comparative Study of the Law of Criminal Procedure in NATO Countries Under the NATO Status of Forces Agreement," 35 *North Carolina Law Review* 358–379 (1957).

Snyder, E. A. "The N.A.T.O. Status of Forces Agreement in England," 19 *Federal Bar Journal* 136–151 (1959).

Tanjuakio, R. D. "The U.S.-P.I. Military Bases Agreement," 30 *Philippine Law Journal* 599–618 (1955).

[Memorandum] U.S. Department of Justice. "International Law and the Status of Forces Agreement," 99 *Congressional Record* 8762–8769 (1953).

Valeros, Antonio. "Jurisdiction of Philippine Courts Over Personnel of the United States Military Reservations in the Philippines," 4 *University of the East Law Journal* 18–36 (1961).

PUBLIC DOCUMENTS

CINCPAC Representative Philippines and Commander U.S. Naval Forces Philippines. *CINCPACREP PHIL/COMNAVPHIL Instruction 5820.1B*. 7 Sep. 1965.

Constitution of the Philippines. Manila: Bureau of Printing, 1966.

Official Opinions of the Attorneys General of the United States. Vols. 6, 24, 26, 28, 41.

Philippine Islands, Attorney General. *Official Opinions of the Attorney-General of the Philippine Islands*. Vol. 1.

Philippines. *Official Gazette*. Vols. 1, 10, 35, 36, 41, 43–58.

Supreme Court of the Philippines. *Rules of Court in the Philippines*. Supplement to Volume 58, *Official Gazette*. Manila: Bureau of Printing, 1962. [Effective, January 1, 1964.]

U.S. *Congressional Record*. Vols. 78, 91–110.

U.S. Department of Defense. *Directive No. 5525.1*. May 5, 1962. Reprinted in U.S. Senate, Subcommittee of the Committee on Armed Services. *Hearings, Operation of Article VII, NATO Status of Forces Treaty*. 87th Cong., 2d Sess., 1962. Pp. 5–21.

—. *JAG Form 66* [Replaces *OCS Form 782*]. 1956–1964.

—. *OCS Form 782*. 1954–1955.

U.S. Department of the Navy. *Laws Relating to the Navy, Annotated*. Washington: Government Printing Office, 1922.

U.S. Department of State. *Department of State Bulletin*. Vols. 1–53.

—. *The Philippines*. Washington: Government Printing Office, 1951.

—. *The World War*. Supplement 2 of *Papers Relating to the Foreign Relations of the United States: 1918*. Washington: Government Printing Office, 1933.

U.S. High Commissioner to the Philippines. *Third Annual Report of the United States High Commissioner to the Philippine Islands to the President and Congress of the United States Covering the Calendar Year 1938 and the First Six Months of 1939*. Washington: Government Printing Office, 1943.

U.S. House of Representatives, Committee on Foreign Affairs. *Hearings, Status of Forces Agreements*. Part 1, 84th Cong., 1st Sess., 1955; Part II, 84th Cong., 2d Sess., 1956.

U.S. Senate. *Charges of Cruelty, Etc., to the Natives of the Philippines*. Document 205, 57th Cong., 1st Sess., 1901–1902.

U.S. Senate, Committee on Armed Services. *Hearings, On the Case of United States Army Specialist Third Class William S. Girard...* 85th Cong., 1st Sess., 1957.

U.S. Senate, Subcommittee of the Committee on Armed Services. *Hearings, Operation of Article VII, NATO Status of Forces Treaty*. 84th Cong., 1st Sess., 1955.

—. *Hearings, Operation of Article VII...* 84th Cong., 2d Sess., 1956.

—. *Hearings, Operation of Article VII...* 85th Cong., 1st Sess., 1957.

—. *Hearings, Operation of Article VII...* 85th Cong., 2d Sess., 1958.

—. *Hearings, Operation of Article VII...* 86th Cong., 1st Sess., 1959.

—. *Hearings, Operation of Article VII...* 86th Cong., 2d Sess., 1960.

—. *Hearings, Operation of Article VII...* 87th Cong., 1st Sess., 1961.

—. *Hearings, Operation of Article VII...* 87th Cong., 2d Sess., 1962.

—. *Hearings, Operation of Article VII...* 88th Cong., 1st Sess., 1963.

—. *Hearings, Operation of Article VII...* 88th Cong., 2d Sess., 1964.

—. *Hearings, Operation of Article VII...* 89th Cong., 1st Sess., 1965.
U.S. *Statutes at Large.* Vols. 32, 39, 47, 48, 58, 64, 70.
U.S. War Department. *Acts of the First Philippine Legislature.* Vol. 9 of *Annual Reports of the War Department for the Fiscal Year Ended June 30, 1908.* Washington: Government Printing Office, 1908.
—. *Acts of the Philippine Commission.* Vol. 11 of *Annual Reports... 1902.* (57th Cong., 2d Sess.; House Document 2.) Washington: Government Printing Office, 1902.
—. *Acts of the Philippine Commission.* Vol. 8 of *Annual Reports... 1903.* (58th Cong., 2d Sess.; House Document 2.) Washington: Government Printing Office, 1903.
—. *Annual Reports of the Secretary of War 1899–1903.* Washington: Government Printing Office, 1904.
—. *Public Laws and Resolutions Passed by the Philippine Commission.* Vol. 1, Part 10 of *Annual Reports of the War Department for the Fiscal Year Ended June 30, 1901.* Washington: Government Printing Office, 1901.
—. *Report of the Philippine Commission.* Vol. 7 of *Annual Reports... 1901.* (57th Cong., 1st Sess.; House Document 2.) Washington: Government Printing Office, 1901.
—. *Report of the Philippine Commission.* Vol. 10 of *Annual Reports... 1902.* (57th Cong., 2d Sess.; House Document 2.) Washington: Government Printing Office, 1902.
—. *Report of the Philippine Commission.* Vol. 7 of *Annual Reports... 1903.* (58th Cong., 2d Sess.; House Document 2.) Washington: Government Printing Office, 1903.
—. *Report of the Philippine Division.* Vol. 3 of *Annual Reports... 1909.* Washington: Government Printing Office, 1910.
—. *Report of the Philippine Division.* Vol. 3 of *Annual Reports... 1910.* Washington: Government Printing Office, 1910.
—. *Report of the Major General Commanding the Army.* Vol. 5 of *Annual Reports... 1899.* (56th Cong., 1st Sess.; House Document 2.) Washington: Government Printing Office, 1899.
—. *Report of the Military Governor of the Philippine Islands on Civil Affairs.* Vol. 1 of *Annual Reports... 1900.* (56th Cong., 2d Sess.; House Document 2.) Washington: Government Printing Office, 1900.
—. *Reports of the Secretary of War, Chief of Staff, Adjutant General, Inspector General, and Judge-Advocate-General.* Vol. 1 of *Annual Reports... 1903.* (58th Cong., 2d Sess.; House Document 2.) Washington: Government Printing Office, 1903.
U.S. War Department, Office of the Judge-Advocate General of the Army. *The Military Laws of the United States with Supplement Showing Changes to March 4, 1907.* 4th ed. Washington: Government Printing Office, 1908.
—. *The Military Laws of the United States.* 8th ed. Washington: Government Printing Office, 1939.
—. *Supplement III to the Military Laws of the United States 8th ed. 1939.* Washington: Government Printing Office, 1945.

TREATIES AND AGREEMENTS

General

(Chronological Order)

Great Britain-France agreement of December 15, 1915. U.S. Department of State. *The World War.* Supplement 2 of *Papers Relating to the Foreign Relations of the United States: 1918.* Washington: Government Printing Office, 1933. Pp. 737–738.
United States-France agreement of January 14, 1918. U.S. Department of State. *The World War.* Supplement 2 of *Papers Relating...: 1918.* Pp. 735–737.

United States-Belgium agreement of September 6, 1918. U.S. Department of State. *The World War*. Supplement 2 of *Papers Relating...: 1918*. Pp. 747–748, 751.

Great Britain-Iraq agreement of October 10, 1922. *Great Britain Treaty Series*. No. 17 (1925).

Great Britain-Egypt agreement of August 26, 1936. *Great Britain Treaty Series*. No. 6 (1937).

United States-Great Britain agreement of July 27, 1942. U.S. Department of State. *Executive Agreement Series*. No. 355 (1942).

United States-India agreement of September 29 and October 10, 1942. *Executive Agreement Series*. No. 392 (1942).

United States-Egypt agreement of March 2, 1943. *Executive Agreement Series*. No. 356 (1943).

United States-China agreement of May 21, 1943. *Executive Agreement Series*. No. 360 (1943).

United States-Belgium agreement (with respect to the Belgium Congo) of August 4, 1943. *Executive Agreement Series*. No. 395 (1943).

Great Britain-China agreement of July 7, 1945. 14 *United Nations Treaty Series* 445 (1948).

North Atlantic Treaty Organization. Status of Forces Agreement. Signed at London June 19, 1951; entered into force for the United States August 23, 1953. 4 *United States Treaties and Other International Acts* [*UST*] 1792; *Treaties and Other International Acts Series* [*TIAS*] 2846.

Security Treaty [United States-Japan]. Signed at San Francisco September 8, 1951; ratifications exchanged April 28, 1952. 3 *UST* 3329; *TIAS* 2491.

Administrative Agreement under Article III of the Security Treaty, and Exchange of Notes. Signed at Tokyo February 28, 1952; entered into force April 28, 1952. 3 *UST* 3341; *TIAS* 2492.

Protocol to Amend Article XVII of the Administrative Agreement under Article III of the Security Treaty between the United States of America and Japan. Signed at Tokyo September 29, 1953; entered into force October 29, 1953. 4 *UST* 1846; *TIAS* 2848.

Agreement Relating to the Stationing of United States Armed Forces in the Netherlands, with Annex. Exchange of Notes at The Hague August 13, 1954; entered into force November 16, 1954. 6 *UST* 103; *TIAS* 3174.

Agreement Relating to Military Bases in Libya, with Memorandum of Understanding. Signed at Benghazi September 9, 1954; entered into force October 30, 1954. 5 *UST* 2449; *TIAS* 3107.

Memorandum of Understanding Relating to Jurisdiction over United States Armed Forces [in Libya] under the Agreement of September 9, 1954. Signed at Tripoli February 24, 1955; entered into force February 24, 1955; applicable from October 30, 1954. 7 *UST* 2051; *TIAS* 3607.

Agreement Concerning the Status of United States Forces in Greece. Signed at Athens September 7, 1956; entered into force September 7, 1956. 7 *UST* 2555; *TIAS* 3649.

Agreement on the Legal Status of Soviet Troops Temporarily Stationed in Poland. Signed at Warsaw December 17, 1956; in force February 27, 1957. 52 *American Journal of International Law* [*AJIL*] 221–227 (1958).

Agreement Concerning Questions Connected with the Presence of Soviet Forces on East German Territory. Signed at Berlin March 12, 1957; in force April 27, 1957. 52 *AJIL* 210–215 (1958).

Agreement on the Legal Status of the Soviet Forces Temporarily Present on the Territory of the Hungarian People's Republic. Signed at Budapest, May 27, 1957. 52 *AJIL* 215–221 (1958).

Agreement for the Establishment of Loran Transmitting Station [in Nicaragua]. Signed at Managua September 5, 1958; entered into force September 5, 1958. 9 *UST* 1206; *TIAS* 4106.

Treaty of Mutual Cooperation and Security, with Agreed Minute and Exchange of Notes [United States-Japan]. Signed at Washington January 19, 1960; entered into force June 23, 1960. 11 *UST* 1632; *TIAS* 4509.

Agreement under Article VI of the Treaty of Mutual Cooperation and Security Regarding Facilities and Areas and the Status of United States Armed Forces in Japan, with Agreed Minutes and Exchange of Notes. Signed at Washington January 19, 1960; entered into force June 23, 1960. 11 *UST* 1652; *TIAS* 4510.

Agreement Concerning United States Defense Areas in the Federation of the West Indies, with Annex and Memorandums of Understandings, Agreed Minute, and Exchange of Notes. Signed at Port-of-Spain February 10, 1961; entered into force February 10, 1961. *TIAS* 4734.

Agreement Concerning the Status of United States Forces in Australia. Signed at Canberra May 9, 1963; entered into force May 9, 1963. *TIAS* 5349.

Agreement Concerning Facilities and Areas and the Status of United States Armed Forces in Korea, with Agreed Minutes, Agreed Understandings and Exchange of Letters. Signed at Seoul July 9, 1966; entered into force May 9, 1967. *TIAS* 6127.

United States-Philippines

(Chronological Order)

Treaty of General Relations, and Protocol. Signed at Manila July 4, 1946; entered into force October 22, 1946. 61 *Statutes at Large* 1174; *TIAS* 1568.

Agreement Concerning Military Bases, and Exchange of Notes. Signed at Manila March 14, 1947; entered into force March 26, 1947. 61 *Statutes at Large* 4019; *TIAS* 1775.

Economic and Technical Cooperation Agreement. Signed at Manila April 27, 1951; entered into force May 21, 1951. 3 *UST* 3707; *TIAS* 2498.

Mutual Defense Treaty. Signed at Washington August 30, 1951; entered into force August 27, 1952. 3 *UST* 3947; *TIAS* 2529.

Agreement Relating to the Immediate Release to the Philippine Authorities of Two Areas Occupied by the Manila Air Station. Exchange of Notes at Manila January 27, 1958; entered into force January 27, 1958. 9 *UST* 131; *TIAS* 3985.

Agreement Relating to the Relinquishment to the Philippines of the Remaining Area of the Manila Air Station and the Deactivation of the Manila Air Base. Exchange of Notes at Manila July 31, 1958; entered into force July 31, 1958. 9 *UST* 1075; *TIAS* 4083.

Agreement for the Establishment of a Mutual Defense Board and the Assignment of Philippine Military Liaison Officers to United States Bases in the Philippines. Exchange of Notes at Manila May 15, 1958; entered into force May 15, 1958. 9 *UST* 547; *TIAS* 4033.

Memorandum of Agreement of August 14, 1959. 3 *Philippine International Law Journal* 438–442 (1964).

Memorandum of Agreement of October 12, 1959. 3 *Philippine International Law Journal* 442–445 (1964).

Agreement Relating to the Relinquishment of Olongapo and Adjacent Areas, with Annex. Exchange of Notes at Manila December 7, 1959; entered into force December 7, 1959. 10 *UST* 2169; *TIAS* 4388.

Agreement Relating to the Establishing of a Peace Corps Program in the Republic of the Philippines. Exchange of Notes signed at Manila October 11 and 31, 1961; entered into force October 31, 1961. 12 *UST* 1699; *TIAS* 4889.

Agreement Relating to Criminal Jurisdiction Arrangement, Amending the Agreement of March 14, 1947, as Amended. Exchange of Notes at Manila August 10, 1965; entered into force August 10, 1965. 16 *UST* 1090; *TIAS* 5851.

Agreement Relating to the Relinquishment and the Acquisition of Certain Base Lands in the Philippines by the United States, with Annex. Exchange of Notes at Manila December 22, 1965; entered into force December 22, 1965. *TIAS* 5824.

UNPUBLISHED MATERIALS

Cho, Sung Yoon. "Jurisdiction Over Foreign Forces in Japan, 1945–1960." Unpublished Ph.D. dissertation, Tulane University, 1964.

—. "Criminal Jurisdiction Over Visiting Friendly Armed Forces, with Special Reference to Anglo-American Practice." Unpublished M.A. thesis, Tulane University, 1957.

Golay, Frank H. "Philippine Foreign Policy: Security or Identity." A paper prepared for the Asian Society and Association for Asian Studies Conference on "The Foreign Policies of the Southeast Asian States," New York, May 14–15, 1965.

Meyer, Milton Walker. "A Diplomatic History of the Philippine Republic." Unpublished Ph.D. dissertation, Stanford University, 1959.

INDEX

Joseph W. Dodd

Criminal Jurisdiction under the United States-Philippine Military Bases Agreement

A Study in Conjurisdictional Law

Martinus Nijhoff / The Hague

Columbia University-School of Law-Project on International Procedure.

Editor Hans Smit.

1. Ginsburg, Ruth Bader, and Anders Bruzelius, Civil procedure in Sweden. 1965. LXXXIV and 491 pp. Cloth. Guilders 63.—
2. Cappelletti, M., and Joseph M. Perillo, Civil procedure in Italy. 1965. XXXII and 451 pp. Cloth. Guilders 54.—
3. International co-operation in litigation: Europe. 1965. XXXIV and 486 pp. Cloth. Guilders 58.50
4. Herzog, Peter, with the collaboration of Martha Weser, Civil procedure in France. 1967. XLI and 708 pp. Cloth. Guilders 72.—

Deener, David R., The United States Attorneys General and international law. 1957. XVI and 416 pp. Cloth. Guilders 26.50

Degan, V. D., L'interprétation des accords en droit international. 1963. XI and 176 pp. Guilders 16.20

Eek, Hilding, The Swedish conflict of laws. 1965. XV and 304 pp. Cloth. Guilders 29.—

Ellert, Robert B., Nato "Fair Trial" safeguards. Precursor to an international bill of procedural rights. 1963. VI and 89 pp. Guilders 9.40

Foda, Ezzeldin, The projected Arab Court of Justice. A study in regional jurisdiction with specific reference to the Muslim law of nations. Presentation by A. H. Badawi, Vice President, International Court of Justice. 1957. XIV and 252 pp. Cloth. Guilders 19.—

Garcia Mora, Manuel R., International responsibility for hostile acts of private persons against foreign states. 1962. XVII and 207 pp. Guilders 20.—

Gormley, W. P., The procedural status of the individual before international and supranational tribunals. 1966. XVI and 206 pp. Guilders 27.—

Gorove, Stephen, Law and politics of the Danube. Interdisciplinary study. With a foreword by Hans Kohn. 1964. V and 171 pp. With 1 map. Guilders 20.75

Hashem, Hisham R., Arab contract of employment. Conflict and concord. A comparative study. 1964. XXXII and 297 pp. Cloth. Guilders 30.45

Hoyt, Edwin C., The unanimity rule in the revision of treaties. A re-examination. With a foreword by Philip C. Jessup. 1959. XII and 264 pp. Guilders 21.85

Kahng, Tae Jin, Law, politics and the security council. An inquiry into the handling of legal questions involved in international disputes and situations. With a foreword by Leland M. Goodrich. 1964. XIV and 252 pp. Guilders 27.95

GPSR Compliance

The European Union's (EU) General Product Safety Regulation (GPSR) is a set of rules that requires consumer products to be safe and our obligations to ensure this.

If you have any concerns about our products, you can contact us on ProductSafety@springernature.com

In case Publisher is established outside the EU, the EU authorized representative is:

Springer Nature Customer Service Center GmbH
Europaplatz 3
69115 Heidelberg, Germany

Batch number: 10830943

Printed by Printforce, the Netherlands